JESSICA BROADWAY

A Journey to Raising Brave Hearts

For Permission requests, write to Jessica Broadway via email at

www.jessicabroadway.com

First edition

ISBN: 978-1-7363720-0-5

Editing by Jeanette Quinton-Zorn
Cover art by Pro_Designzz
Typesetting by Jeanette Quinton-Zorn

This book was professionally typeset on Reedsy.
Find out more at reedsy.com

For Mom and Dad, thank you for raising Brave Hearts.

Honor the living, remember the dead.
Cheers to choosing life

Contents

Preface

Dear {Brave} Heart,

Raising Brave Hearts is a personal journey
about hope and rising out of the ashes of what holds us back.

I am addressing you as "Brave Heart" because we already have a connection if you picked up this book. You already have a Brave Heart inside you. Raising Brave Hearts is what we will do together, and you have everything you need for the journey.

Thank you for saying YES to your first {AND} moment.
When you say YES - <u>Y</u>ou <u>E</u>ncourage <u>S</u>uccess.

{AND} moments are when you have reasons not too but do it anyway. You are living your busy life <u>AND</u> taking the time to join me on a journey. Your sacrifice of time is not wasted on me. Thank you. Raising Brave Hearts is a soul song, but don't worry, I won't sing to you. It's about the truth: my truth and yours; These forgotten truths living deep inside us, and when we most need them, God uses others to whisper those truths back to us.

Maybe you feel like you've got this life. You're doing great. Well, that was me until my world completely shifted, and I saw a world I didn't recognize—a world where people were afraid to live and where they were pretending to be OK with it. In front of me was a world where people didn't forgive, and they loved with conditions of performance. This saddened me deeply. I suppose I started seeing this in the world because I was living it. I had lost my way and began living in the stories of what I thought life should be like, and I was angry it wasn't that way. And the craziness of this? At the time, I had no idea. Ignorance was bliss. I was playing my role like everyone else, and YOU would have never known the difference.

One event. One major event and my life turned upside down. My dad died. It jolted me into a completely different way of viewing the world. I couldn't juggle all things, keep smiling, keep doing. I didn't want his death to be another thing I survived and just another badge of hard knocks. I realized the impact of loss in my life and how I could not recognize the grief. Once you notice what grief looks like, you can't help but see it everywhere. You can't help but notice the way it holds people back without awareness in every area of life. In business, relationships, weight loss, and even in their relationship with God.

My way out was to start intentionally creating a life I had long wished existed. There is much more to life than overcoming and surviving. When I started this new way of "creating what I wish existed" on purpose, I discovered it takes a great deal of courage. Rising from the ashes of what holds you back requires a Brave Heart. It also requires a commitment to authentic living. Fiercely motivated to move beyond the experiences I had allowed to hold me back, I poured over many resources, searching for the fix. During that process I discovered one of my superpowers is making hard things user-friendly. It's hard to understand grief, much less recognize it. It's hard to forgive, to understand grace and God's love. It's hard to overcome hard things. What if you could do all this in an easily understandable way? In sharing my journey with you, I want to take the hard stuff and make it user-friendly, creating moments you say, "Me too!" Moments which empower you to embrace your own Brave Heart.

* * *

When you're reading this, I invite you to be honest with yourself, to gut check often, and be open to the possibility for growth. Brave Hearts tell the truth. It's a necessary step to empowerment.

Realizing this freedom for myself, I desperately want it for everyone, so I wrote Raising Brave Hearts. The first of what I hope to be many books about what it takes to embrace your Brave Heart in all areas of life. In sharing my grief, forgiveness, and healing journey, I want to inspire you to embrace a state of acknowledgment of the loss in your own life. Be full of hope for the future, love others without needing to fix them first, and free yourself from the burden of opinion - which you will learn is not the same as deciding to not care what other people think.

These are my stories, the lessons I've learned through living. Some I learned in the moment, and some the impact was not fully realized until much later. I hope you find yourself in my stories and you can say, "Me too" at least once. I'm the storyteller and the musician, but you make it all possible. YOU are the instrument of this music. We can't change the world if we don't take action. We do our very best work when we work together, and together is my favorite place to be!

Once upon a time I had this overwhelming pull and a quiet whisper to my soul, "It's time to tell the story." This book is in obedience and fulfillment of that calling. I also have created some space for you to reflect throughout the book. Enjoy and thank you for being here.

Are you ready?

Jessica

P.S. *Also, please note I talk like I write, SO grammar police, I love you. Thank you for protecting the English language. I'm inviting you to have a conversation, not read a dissertation.

Acknowledgement

If you're reading this, you're part of the journey. The journey of "Raising Brave Hearts," so thank you!

This has been in the works for years, and what a beautiful process it has been. The lessons, the people, and watching myself grow each time I was frustrated with the lack of progress. The frustration turned into gratitude for the missing pieces revealed through the struggle. I knew from the beginning Raising Brave Hearts would be the work of many and when it was finished, people would say, "I helped bring that to life." People read for me, edited, shared their stories, cheered me on, believed in me, challenged me, designed for me, and yes, even rebuked my ideas. This book coming to fruition reflects many people doing a little bit and making a HUGE impact for good.

I could not have accomplished this without others' kindness, those who wanted to pay it forward. Thank you all for helping make this dream come true.

Susan, my mentor, and friend. "Consider it pure joy, my brothers and sisters, whenever you face trials of many kinds" James 1:2. You stand in the presence of trials and shine joyfully for all the world. Finding the fun and passing the joy. Thank you for believing in me and guiding me on the journey to publishing.

Jeanette, my Editor and mentor. Thank you for following your intuition, for taking a leap with me. You took this first-time author under your wing and have flawlessly guided me through the journey. Our journey together was only made possible because it was always meant to be. I used to feel like I was late in following through, but now I know I was right on time to meet you. I am not sure you will ever know quite how many things had to go wrong for me to find you. Thank you for helping turn messes into messages and for believing in Raising Brave Hearts. Through you, God has shown me how faithful He is in providing more than we ever imagine possible.

Supper club, I remember the first time we were gathered at the table, setting intentions for full, meaningful relationships based on total honesty. I also remember the feelings I had in the moment I spoke out and shared I wanted to start Living Forward Workshops. I wondered if you would all think I was weird or the dream was too big. You didn't. You encouraged, sacrificed, you trusted me enough to be my very first workshop. You all became my safe place to dream. Thank you for saying YES to all the adventures of friendship, even when it's hard.

I

Part One

It's the "chicken or the egg moment!"
It's the journey to clarity. Is this really all life prepared us for?
This moment?
*Or does '**This Moment**' give you clarity on your whole life?*
The answer is always both.

One

Introduction

It's the "chicken or the egg moment!" It's the journey to clarity. Is this really all life prepared us for? **This moment**? Or does **this moment** give you clarity on your whole life? The answer is *always* both.

My friend Joann taught me to notice and wonder. Well, maybe she didn't teach me, but she did, however, most definitely give me words to explain what I do. Hearing her explain my process for life was exciting. She said, "You're good at noticing and wondering." It was the first time I'd heard this concept. And you know what? She was right! This skill, it's a big part of what makes me, me. I notice the world and wonder how I can make it better.

**"I love to stand in the gap for others,
holding on to the belief it is possible to create the life you wish
existed."**

This book will show you there is freedom in honesty. And in honesty lies the hard truth, which is what our souls crave to stay in alignment. Denying the truth feeds an illusion we are not "good enough." I do not presume if you are reading this, you are unhappy. Just if given the space, you too might discover some hopes, dreams, and expectations for relationships, your careers, or for yourself you have yet to acknowledge are possible to create. To *love* ALL your life.

After my dad died, I found myself very critical. Angry, even. As if a great injustice had occurred. I was not angry at God. Just mad at the world. It seemed so broken. Everywhere I looked, I saw people hurting, grieving. They had lost the sparkle in their eyes too. Someone or something had stolen their joy. The injustice for me was it didn't seem fair. How could it be fair a man full of life, joy, grit, and grace was gone? In his place were so many who had given up. Survivors with heartbeats who had forgotten how *to live*. This idea of being detached from your heart is when we experience pain and build a tiny wall, "Just so I can heal." Then, instead of taking down the wall, you just keep building it. Before long, it's business as usual, and instead of noticing you can no longer see over the wall, you just create a life behind the wall where you detach from yourself and others.

For the first time in my life, I recognized grief. I grieved the grief. It broke my heart differently. I saw not only were others grieving, but many didn't recognize their own grief. They were asleep and had settled for a mediocre life. Surrendering hopes and dreams for the price of admission to a life where they are just "hanging in there." Drawing lines around what is *lovable*, self-righteously judging each other. *Why?!* Why were they just hanging in there? Why do we find it so easy to hate for no reason and near impossible to choose to love for no reason?

Noticing this and wondering how to fix it was the beginning of my journey. BUT...first, I had to come to terms with my own grief. I needed to acknowledge all the ways I had allowed grief to impact how I saw myself, my value, relationships, and career. I needed to come full circle to help others do the same. The journey to completion takes a Brave Heart. It takes grit and grace. It's a paradigm shift. So, you may ask, why can't I just leave well enough alone, stay in my own lane? Well, one of my beliefs is we are better **together**. ALWAYS. The problem so many of us face is we aren't free to show up in the world. The more I studied grief and wrestled with my own, this concept became clearer. It was the same thing over and over again. A loss we were ill-equipped to deal with changed how we see the world, how we see ourselves in it, and how we relate to others.

In the coming chapters, I will share the journey with you to raising my own brave heart. Share tips with you and distinctions you can apply in your own life. Taking hard topics and making them user-friendly. Finally, maybe by the end of writing this, my word processor will understand I mean BRAVE HEART, not braveheart. You'll have discovered what YOUR Brave Heart looks like, too, and join me in raising a community of Brave Hearts who notice the world and wonder how they can impact it.

During our journey together, I will share with you the untidy bits. The best way for me to accomplish this was to pull the text from my journals in the moments I was processing and then reflect on having come through it. I hope this creates a connection, and although our stories are very different, you can say "me too."

**"Life is built in the 'AND' moments.
Those moments we choose to rise and embrace our Brave Hearts."**

*Embracing life together,
we can raise a community of
Brave Hearts.*

Two

The Rebuild

"Get in the car kids," she announced.

I remember us all loading into the Peugeot. We are going to get your Dad's car. Get Dad's car? But he already had one. Obedient yet confused, we piled in the car. I'm certain there was whining about having to go somewhere and fighting over who was in the 3rd row, the typical kid stuff. I don't remember the daily grumblings, but as a parent myself now, I realize it comes with the territory. Kids love to tell you how they feel about stuff.

Our weekly chores as kids were to rotate who cleaned the car out. It was a miserable job. I always hated it starting out, but I was proud of the work by the time I was finished. It's the one chore I remember always being worth it. A space that was clean. However, in the moment of announcing the new car, it was just ANOTHER car to clean, and for a kid, it was like a doomsday sentence. I remember the drive was long, we dropped my dad off, and he made a roadside transaction. He was now the proud new owner of a 1969 Mach 1 Mustang. Learning to state car facts like make, model, and horsepower would later earn me many brownie points with teenage boys. But back then, I only knew what it was called because of how proud Dad looked when he said it. The way his face lit up talking about it meant it must be important.

In truth, it was a bit of a Junker, but he had a vision for it. Most of the Mustang's days were spent in the garage occupying lots of Dad's time and seemed to make only annual appearances for Guy Fawkes Night, a night where roaring mufflers and shock less tires were welcome. He used to give joy rides around the church parking lot. He would spin out, floor it, and off we would go.

Dad used to race cars in his "teen years" as he would tell us. He had an old T-bucket he rebuilt and would "Race on the streets of Houston Texas."If you just cut to the race scene in the movie Grease, so did I. I imagine many of my dad's stories playing out just like this movie. He was, as he put it, kind of a scrappy kid. Getting in fights, smoking, and racing cars on the weekend. Until a girl invited him to church. He said he went for the girl and stayed because of Jesus. He would later give his life to Christ and begin a life-long mission, sharing the gospel around the world.

The Mustang stayed pretty low key in our family in those early years, other than its annual reveal at the bonfires on Guy Fawkes. Dad always had a thing for classic cars, and car shows were his jam. Car shows weren't as popular in Scotland, so you can imagine his delight when we moved to the States. There is practically a car show every weekend, somewhere. The Mustang would get more joy rides than ever when we moved to Florida. I remember him working so hard on it, driving it for a few weeks, and then having to park it again. He seemed to be working on it all the time. I do remember thinking, "Why do you have a car that breaks down all the time?" If you know anything about the car-loving world, having a car you are working on is very different from a car that breaks down. Albeit I couldn't tell the difference in my teen years, they were the same thing to me. JUNKERS.

Nevertheless, the Mustang got garage space. It got time, love, and shaped a childhood for us. I learned how to change a brake line, pump a line, brake pads, radiators, mufflers, change the oil. It certainly returned in memories what Dad gave it in love. It bore witness to heartaches, confessions, lessons, and laughter. It was a good car that "almost never" worked.

* * *

One particular day my sister was riding her bike and lost control. She headed into the garage at an alarming speed, crashing and skidding the bike alongside the Mustang, leaving a decent scratch. Her face was horrified. She immediately started crying, not from injury but in fear of how Dad would handle the newly acquired scratch in his car. He came running right to her.

"Are you ok, sweetheart?" Completely ignoring his question, she squealed out through her tears,

"I'm sorry about the car, Daddy."

"The car!" He chuckled.

"I can fix the car, but I can't get another you." The relief on her face; on my face. It is my favorite memory, learning people matter. You can get more things, but not more people.

In middle school, I entered the age of embarrassment. Not actually embarrassed, just pretending like I was.

NOTE TO SELF: When Landon starts rolling his eyes. He's only pretending he's too big for a hug, I'll remind myself.

* * *

The Mustang was in it's prime at this point. At school, boys were beginning to really like cars, so it began—my love-hate relationship with being dropped off at school in the Mustang. I only wanted to be dropped off if I could guarantee a certain 8th-grade boy would see it because it's the only time I existed in his world; and would almost guarantee me thirty seconds of acknowledgment. I know, I know. My adult self is shaking her head. This boy hung out at a certain table in a commons area - he was a bus rider, so timing was everything. I couldn't get there too early, and if I were too late, he would already have moved to homeroom stations, to which I had the unfortunate luck of being on the other side of the building from his.

You realize, of course, I could tell my dad NONE of this. As far as he knew, he was just the cool Dad who dropped his kid off. That was until he decided to turn the car off to yell out the window his favorite parting greeting. Yeah, his finest Dad moment. We make the turn into the carline; he gives the extra throttle to rev the engine. At this point, there are no mufflers on the Mustang, so it's VERY loud. He creeps up to the drop off-site. I spot the perfect place and yell, "This is it. Stop here!"

You can't really hear much over the loud engine, which I'm thankful for because Dad had a habit of yelling out eye-roll-worthy statements. Today I just wanted out of the car. Everyone was now looking our way, and the crowd had come to an unusual hush. The hush was undetectable in the midst of the roaring engine. I didn't realize such silence existed until he killed the engine. I don't know if it was because he forgot to say it, or I didn't respond; but as I made my way across the commons, he killed the engine. At first, I thought it was another breakdown. I would have been humiliated. A loud fixer-upper is cool. A broke down fixer-upper, your Dad had to get towed! Well, it's not! I remember spinning around to assess the situation, only to see Dad leaned across the passenger's seat, stretching to the open window to yell.

"Remember who you are and whose you are, sweetheart. Have a good day."

I wish I could pause this moment and just repeat it over and over again. I wish I had run back to the car and hugged him and said, "I love you too, thank you for being such a good Dad. Thank you for loving me enough to stop the car and making sure I know where I belong. Thank you." Instead, I just rolled my eyes and darted for the nearest door. All-day, I fielded questions about, "What did your dad say to you this morning?" "Does he say that all the time?" "Your dad is kinda weird."

You know the ironic part about that day? I actually loved hearing him say those words. I felt loved and important. Important enough to have someone call out to me. It's one of my first memories of being told,

"Remember who you are and whose you are,"

Though the more I learn about the things which impact you, the more I understand it was likely something he said ALL the time. It didn't connect until it involved all of my senses. That was the day it became a core memory for me. I would now hear it every time he said it.

That phrase:

Protected me when I left the house on prom night,

"Remember who you are and whose you are," *he yelled*

It comforted me when my heart was jarred, and I couldn't see myself,

"Remember who you are and whose you are," *he whispered.*

It revived me when I was tired,

"Remember who you are and whose you are," *he challenged.*

It created hope when he drew his last breath.

"Remember who you are and whose you are," *I whispered.*

* * *

It won't be the Mustang that embarrasses my kids. I'm not sure what my thing will be, perhaps my love for skipping with them, or elaborate costumes and red lipstick. I do know this. I can't wait for the day they remember what I have said since they were small.

"Remember who you are and whose you are, sweetheart."

Remember WHO you are and WHOSE you are.
Thanks for instilling that in me, Dad.

"Remember who you are and whose you are." *(Dean English)*

Three

Confetti Full of Grace

*T*he question: "What does **Who You Are and Whose You Are** mean?"

As I said in Chapter One, it had meant different things at different times to me. As a young girl, it mostly meant I'm Jessica, not Jess, Jessie, or another shortcut to addressing me as less than who I was, which was Jessica. My dad also had the habit of correcting everyone who would take liberties with my name. Your name is the first thing you begin to identify with. It is how we first become known. It's our response when asked, "Who are you?".

The 'whose' part was rooted in the identity I was my parent's child. I knew what was expected, the price tag of belonging to our family. This elementary understanding of 'whose' you are kept me out of trouble gave me the pride to say I'm an English. My parents paved the way and gave us a legacy of pride in our family. I belonged to a family who loved me and loved others—a legacy of grace. Growing up in Scotland, to share who I belonged to was to claim American parents and grandparents. I was the cool kid whose Grandparents lived in America; it was exotic to travel every other summer to America for months.

Following these long summers in America, we would return to brisk

Scotland sporting deep tans and trendy American accents. When I was twelve, we moved to America. Then I became 'The Tourist.' The foreign student who said, "quite nice," called cookies, biscuits, and most hilarious of my awkward social adjustments was calling erasers... rubbers. Kids had a field day with that. 7th grade was tough. In all honesty, though, I didn't mind so much. It gave me some momentary street cred. Knowing stuff other kids didn't, mysterious and like a shiny new penny.

When I began writing about the events which shaped me and cultivated my Brave Heart, I felt the need to share all the battles. Digging up dirt, like the mess, was what gave me credentials to share. In reflection of my story, my mountain of stuff to overcome seemed like an anthill in comparison to what I know about others' journeys. Here's the deal. Your struggle will always be an anthill to someone else's. There will always be someone "worse off" than you. Opportunities to compare will always be there. They will be waiting to show you how you're not good enough, so don't waste your time.

In learning *'who you are and whose you are,'* you also learn to stop comparing. Be willing to stand in your own space with your own stuff. I have a journey to becoming me, so do you. I have seen a lot, maybe you have or haven't. What you have seen is worth sharing. How you see the world will be as unique as you are, and how I see it is unique to me. The moments we share together is the spark of fire that inspires. I am privileged to notice we are all trying to tell the same story, the story of who we are and whose we are. We all have a desire to be seen, noticed, and contribute. The pain of yesterday cannot be given the freedom to make our choices for tomorrow. Brave Hearts embrace who they are, even the messy parts, and are willing to take the journey to complete the things they wish were better, more, or different in life. The pull to compare ourselves always comes from a place of pain- from a "less than" place.

Comparison is the pain that says, "what if I'm not good enough?" Brave Hearts do the work to complete this pain. Completing our pain is not saying it didn't happen. It's saying goodbye to it and not letting our pain choose for us. C.S. Lewis captures it perfectly when he said,

> *"You can't go back and change the beginning,*
> *but you can start where you are*
> *and change the ending."*

I grew up thinking I could change the world, so I used to spend a good part of the daydreaming about how life will be one day when I've changed the world when I've done all the things I came to do. How life will be ONE DAY, someday when everything is perfect. A lot of time wishing and dreaming. Being a dreamer and taking action, creating what you wish existed is a balance I am practicing, not that I've mastered. If you are like me, a Jill or perhaps you are a Jack, of all trades; Then this part is probably the most important.

Journal entry:
Something amazing happened when I stopped trying to figure out who I was (my accomplishments) and began to discover WHOSE I was and who YOU are. I was a daughter of the King. Gifted to imperfect people to be raised in an imperfect world to show people a glimpse of their true king. To love them unconditionally, with a perfect love which does not insist they perform to be loved. To love myself enough to live imperfectly bold without permission from others. To cherish the things which make us different so we can unite together.

* * *

I was chosen, and so were you. We've all heard you're just like your mother/your father. Whose we are undeniably defines WHO we are. Discovering more about who we belong to shifts the focus from who we are. My journey has been one of embracing abundant grace and throwing it around like confetti.

I discovered this connection one New Year's Eve. I was in search of a fun, family-friendly way to celebrate ringing in the New Year. Our family always had the best New Year's parties. I remember many of them growing

14

up, and I wanted this experience for our kids. This particular year I wanted a unique way. In remembering how New Year parties were growing up, I remembered it was often referred to as Hogmanay. There was an emphasis on first footers - the people first in your home in the New Year, said to bring luck to you. While midnight was not family-friendly, conveniently living in America allowed a six-hour cushy time difference. We scheduled our party for five p.m. - ringing in the New Year at six p.m. This would be the British New year, given the time difference.

I made all the things - all things British. Everyone I invited was chosen to be there because of who they were. I wanted to surround our first moments of the New Year with people we loved. We had gobs of confetti, and as the clock struck six, the confetti exploded into the air in the best slow-motion video ever. The kids and adults scooped up handfuls of confetti for hours, tossing it everywhere. OUR HOUSE WAS FULL of confetti. This moment was more of a blessing than any of us could have ever imagined.

Pieces of this night showed up for YEARS to come. Everyone there managed to carry a little bit of it with them. It was inevitable. It also happens to be quite distinct—little gold foil squares. I have literally mowed the grass and looked down to find a piece of it years later. I have no idea how it keeps showing up. It's the strangest thing, but it warms my heart. For months there were pictures exchanged of all the random places the confetti showed up. Somehow a piece of it showed up at our church building months later. The chaos of confetti flying everywhere was cringe-worthy if you were focused on the mess it was going to make. It was beautiful when you focused on the carefree moment we embraced. Life is not lived in the moments of perfect silence. Those are easy moments to choose. Life is defined by the moments we choose right in the middle of all the noise.

Grace should be spread around like confetti, and forgiveness should be free without restraint.

To my new friends and old, develop who you are by discovering WHOSE you are. To my children- *"Remember who you are and whose you are."* May you read this one day and know you were the sweetest, messiest, and definitely the loudest part of my life. I love you.

I hope you'll write on your mirror. *"Remember who you are and whose you are."* A daily reminder to claim our belonging. We all belong. You might have just forgotten who you are and who you belong to. Take this reminder.

You were fearfully and wonderfully made. You are a treasure more precious than gold, and You belong to the Father of all fathers, and you have been gifted, on loan to the world. I'm thankful He loaned us you.

II

Part Two

I do not presume if you are reading this,
you are unhappy.
Just if given the space, you too might discover some hopes, dreams,
and expectations for relationships, your careers, or for yourself,
you didn't know you had or haven't acknowledged
it is possible to create them.
To love ALL of your life.

Four

Freedom in Honesty

I do not presume that if you are reading this, you are unhappy. Just that if given the space, you too might discover some hopes, dreams, and expectations for relationships, your careers, or for yourself that you didn't know you had or haven't acknowledged that it is possible to create them. To *love* ALL of your life.

This book is not a 'grief book,' although grief and my awareness of it have changed me forever. It took me a long time to say, "My dad died." I preferred to say he passed. We lost him. He went to heaven. I realize now that all those phrases were just ways of avoiding what was really the most painful. Those substitute phrases for the truth didn't make it easier. It was only when I could give a voice to my true pain that I began the process of healing. My truth was, and is, "My dad died, and I miss him."

Saying those words out loud was like my heart said YUP, YUP...that's it! There is freedom in honesty. This part of honesty, the hard truth, it's what our souls crave to stay in alignment. Denying the impact of grief in our life steals value away from the journey we travel. It does nothing but feeds the illusion that we are not "good enough" if we must get help along the way. Our survivor ego we create to avoid loss leaves others' saying, "WOW, I can't believe how strong she is! or "How well she is handling this!" and *not* in a good way. Honoring the journey to becoming you is to share the impact of grief and loss. Sharing the real journey helps others feel like they CAN heal too. Not that they will, but that it's possible.

Beginning to sound a bit hopeless? Nah. We are programmed to believe loss will leave us hopeless because the tools (coping strategies) we've acquired through the years are designed to help us avoid loss rather than embrace it. If you will, let's go back to a very young age, before we experienced any loss. If you remember, we dreamed BIG. Ask any adult what they wanted when they were younger. I bet their dreams were so big they would almost laugh a little when they are reminded of it. Changes in personality and desires aside, the biggest reason we trade in our dreams is that we buy into reality. We took advice from someone that had experienced loss, and they were ill-equipped to deal with it, and it changed them forever. We accepted advice from someone who forgot how to dream. We lost our cheerleaders, who said, "You can do anything you want!" I suppose we bought into it because it felt grown-up. It felt safe in a way, better than the unknown and all that. Shifting, as if hopes and dreams are the only things that have a loss attached to them. We bought the most expensive lie.

The lie that says if you are grounded, realistic, and manage your expectations of others, then you'll not fail, and you'll protect yourself from pain. Have you ever had a moment in slow motion where you asked yourself, "Is this as good as it gets?" You want more, but you are unsure as to how to get it? You might not even know what "IT" is, but you might believe you can't have it. This gain of self-limiting belief, or acceptance without consent, starts to settle way back when we were innocent dreamers. The first time we experience loss and don't know what to do with it, we autocorrect and say to ourselves: "Self, do whatever it takes not to feel like that again!" Our survivor ego is born. Cumulatively, we grow into adults with a whole lotta stuff in our backpacks and not a whole lot of tools to unpack with.

I sense we have all become so cozy protecting ourselves from more loss we've forgotten how to really live and become incredibly disconnected from each other. Our survivor egos propelling us through life, seemingly protecting us, helping us navigate life by finding the best way to avoid more loss. The impact of staying quiet any longer is dire to me. We risk a future enslaved to the "Every man/ woman/child for themselves" mindset. Lonely and craving connection, yet unaware of what we really need, we continue to fill the void with poorly developed coping skills and will inevitably widen the gap. When, what we actually need, are better tools to deal with loss and a safe place to dream again, all wrapped in some Jesus. We need to raise our Brave Hearts.

What I want is more for all of us. I want you to feel fulfilled, to find your voice, and embrace your Brave Heart. To feel empowered to create the life you wish existed in relationships with others and yourself, your careers, and in your spiritual walk.

To make your mark on this world, leaving your unique fingerprint that says, "I showed up to my life."

"Creating hope for people is Honoring the journey, total honesty &
standing in the gap with the belief it's possible for them too."

Five

Raising Our Awareness

G rief is like a baby boy. If you don't know how to handle it, it's gonna pee all over you! Trust me. I know this on both counts.

I tried to run from writing about my grief. Not just my grief about my dad but all of it. I suppose it's because I didn't want to be defined by it. I am aware of all the irony here, and I'll gently remind you I am a work in progress, not a final destination. The last decade has taught me to stop, turn to my grief, and acknowledge it.

This process is an essential part of raising Brave Hearts. To do this, we have to raise our awareness of what grief looks like and where it's showing up. We have to ask ourselves what the losses are behind the pain. Social grooming tells us being brave is when you survive life's challenges, *'Suck it up, Buttercup.'* Busy yourself with life's projects to take your mind off {it} or claim something to replace it in order to avoid being consumed by grief. Being brave is anything BUT avoiding the hard parts of life. To give you a good reading context, I feel it is important to equip you with three areas of awareness heading into this journey together—a mini crash course on what grief really looks like.

First awareness:

Raising your own Brave Heart is, in part, acknowledging that grief exists.

I need to share that my insight into the work of grief is not solely based on my own experience; but years of living, training, learning, and noticing the impact on others. Working through my own journey with loss and others, I understand that grief is more than one word. It's an endless sea of words that flow when you try to explain it. *Grief* is the emotional reaction to the losses we experience. We try avoiding it because we don't understand it. I bet when you hear the word grief, you don't think of someone who just found out they are *cured* of cancer, someone who just had a baby or newly married. Life is ever-changing, and loss is part of daily living, but it's not always negative. A loss occurs even when we have a negative relationship we remove from our lives. We can have mixed feelings. That is grief too. I look back now and cannot believe how unaware I was of the loss one can experience in a week, let alone their whole lives. While some losses have a greater emotional impact than others, a loss is a loss at the end of the day. We all experience it, and arguably it is the ONE thing that has us all saying, "Me too." Sadly, grief is one of the most misunderstood emotions a person can experience, leaving us feeling more misunderstood than ever when we experience it for ourselves.

Second awareness:

Left unrecognized, grief is cumulative over time.

An event that you never recognized as a loss and the emotions attached to it keep stacking up, waiting for the tipping point. Sometimes grief is like one of those movies that begins with the ending, then the rest of the movie is how they got there. A little like this book, I guess. This was very much my experience. Within fourteen months, my pawpaw and my dad both died. Although these were not my first losses, they were a tipping point for me in my awareness of how loss builds over time. Their deaths opened up so much for me. I sought support and discovered a better way to deal with loss than just powering through and stuffing it.

Third awareness-

Is something wrong with me?

Ever find yourself reacting to something "small" that triggers something way bigger? Most people explain this as "opening a can of worms" Y'all, the only reason we avoid opening that can is that we don't have the right tools. Most of us are unaware of the loss that impacts us in our lives and shows up as those tiny adjustments we make in our personalities, thinking we are adjusting to protecting ourselves. Instead of helping you, these little adjustments, these walls of protection have resulted in you being so far off course you wonder, how did I get here.

Maybe you don't even recognize yourself anymore.

Just the other day, I could extend comfort to a friend who was unaware that she was experiencing grief. Instead, she was trying to be strong, keep busy, and overcome her deep desire to be sad about what she was going through. Fighting to stay on the upside of an inevitable downhill slide. After a few short moments of talking, relief washed over her face. "So, nothing is wrong with me?"

"Nope. You just have some broken tools. Let's get you some new ones."

If all this is a little eye-opening, Listen to me. Nothing is wrong with YOU either. What you have experienced is an awareness of loss. The emotional impact (grief) on your life is what has been holding you back. Over the years, I have realized it's not the success we are afraid of. It's the fear of accumulating more loss that really holds us back. Social grooming says we must "get over it" to win. Further implying that we are not good enough, strong enough, or perhaps willing enough if we cannot simply get over it. We have failed to accept loss as part of the journey. This is no one's fault, so don't go blaming your parents for all the ways they didn't give you the right tools or the first person that crushed your dreams. This is just a casualty of life.

Sometimes we get misinformation, and we act on it. The awareness that change needs to occur is the first step. Then we get to build healthy tools and find the people that support us living forward. Naturally, if we have the tools to deal with loss, we no longer fear it. The impact of this shift in our thinking is it is no longer about winning <u>or</u> losing. Life becomes embracing winning AND losing.

It's easy to write about where I am now in the after part. To share with you what I learned, how I did the work. To present to you have learned more and to retell the story a bit tidier. It's brave to be open about where I was, to embrace where I was, and let it stand in its own moment without being ashamed. When we are grieving, it's hard to recognize ourselves. It feels better to keep the lid on the can and present a smile. The problem? - it only feels good for a moment. Over time when the end of the day comes, you feel exhausted, having tried to perform the whole day. It can result in never feeling fully known because you have never been fully honest about the journey you've been on.

Reflection space:

Six

Honoring the journey

❧

*"Don't let the circumstances of the
moment rob you of the moments
in the circumstances."*

J ournal entry: April 30, 2014

*It's been over a year since I wrote anything. It saddens me that grief is
what motivates me to write now. There has been so much this year. The
transition to working from home has been such a blessing, although sometimes you
forget how to hold every day as if it were the only day. We said goodbye to Pawpaw
last April. At the funeral, all I kept hearing was-*

"They sure don't make them like him anymore."

*All I kept thinking was- He's only that man because God was his Lord and Savior,
not because he did anything special or got "lucky in life." He was quite the opposite;
he was a man of the world, whom if you had met in his teens, would have never*

imagined what God saw in him. God won his heart, and when you had coffee with Ken, you had coffee with God. That is what made him THE MAN. At the service, we were blessed by many. Dad did the service and supported us all. His strength was something to be in awe of. Dad has this presence about him, a strength filled with tenderness. I've watched my whole life as he comforted those who were grieving, and now in our moment, he was there. His ability to see the hearts of people has always been one of his gifts. The 2 men I look to for spiritual guidance. When one leader falls, another shall rise into his place—two great men in need of a savior, living out the redemption of the cross. My heart is full of gratitude that I have witnessed such grace.

"Don't let the circumstances of the moment rob you of the moments in the circumstances."

Journal entry June 2014

"It's so great to see you again." We just got to Mom and Dad's a few weeks ago, and that's a phrase I keep hearing. It rolls off their tongues like butter but stings me like a thousand tiny pins. These times are sad times. The kids and I packed up a carload of clothes and toys, grabbed our bags, and set out for a long trek across a couple of states to say our goodbyes to Dad. I'm sitting here now with floods of emotion. This moment is too heavy for me to put into spoken words, so I write.

What does it all mean? What is courage? Overwhelmed with thoughts, I chase all these rabbits in my mind. We have lived more lifetimes than the world put together, it seems—stories filled with GRACE, MERCY, FORGIVENESS, HUMILITY, THANKFULNESS, REDEMPTION.

"The gifts in life aren't in enjoying all the times you got it right. The GIFT is the time to get it right."

27

Don't waste time. Moments slip to infinity, lost forever, discarded for the next moment as if they are never-ending. Then we catch a glimpse of The End and become paralyzed, slaves to the moments. Bound by fear, you will miss life. My God knows my needs, my heart, my desires. He is sufficient to soothe my aching soul. Will, he not give me the moments I need over the moments I want? His grace is sufficient. In Him alone, do we find an eternity of moments. Perspective is the key to life.

* * *

Catch and Release- The time to get it right

I was so incredibly overwhelmed during that time. The overwhelm for me didn't come from what I was experiencing. It was coming from being afraid I would forget something. I was so scared I would forget moments about our time together. I had this overwhelming awareness that time is limited. I felt so rushed to soak up the last moments I couldn't even be present with the moment I was in. The fear that showing up for the present moment would cause me to let go of the previous one. I didn't want to miss a thing. The problem is you can't do that. Living like that causes anxiety, confusion, and is everything but peaceful. We were not designed to live presently in *all the moments at one time*. We were designed to catch the moment in the present, then release it to the past.

We were designed to show up in the moment, free to move to the next moment leaving the pain and regret in the past and embracing the hope of what's to come. To honor the journey of what was by showing up for the moment we are in. In those days, it was difficult not to let the circumstances of why we were gathering- The funerals to rob us of the joy of being present with people we hadn't see in a long time, to celebrate in our sadness. I learned through those moments it is better to honor the living and remember the dead. To find ways to keep choosing life.

. To have the tools to live bravely in the moment without fear of loss. We need a way to release what we are afraid of losing. More than that, we ultimately need to get complete with it. That process varies from person to person. Regardless of how you choose to get complete with the loss in your life, I can share the value I gained from journaling. It became my way of honoring the journey of not only grief but who the real me was without the protective layers. It helped me to step out of my survivor mentality. It gave me a safe place to store the things I didn't know what to do until I found the right tools. It gave my heart and my mind the rest it needed to heal.

Here are a few tips for you in beginning your journaling practice:

1. The thought of journaling can be overwhelming in its own daunting way. When I first started this, I imagined having to start my entries with "Dear Diary." That might have been cool when I was 13, but in my 30's it seems childish. But each to their own when it comes to this. Embrace your style! Just so long as you do it. I wrapped my mind around it by viewing it as telling stories. I just wrote stories about what I noticed and wondered. The good, the bad, the ugly, and most importantly, the honest truth about how I felt.

2. There were times I was exhausted by the details of the day. So, I chose just to write my feelings. It felt more honest, empowering, and releasing. I wrote about the things I wished were better, more, or different... This is important. Make sure your journal entries tell the emotional truth, especially if you come to something you need to get out and you can't remember the details. It matters very little WHAT happened. What does make a difference is the emotion you experienced and what you chose to do next.

3. Create with your entries. Write about limitless dreams. The things you would claim for your life if resources and time were not factors. These creation entries can be about a relationship you dream of having with your spouse, your kids, your career, your desire for spiritual growth. It should all be there. What have you wished for that if, given the right tools, resources, and enough time, you would create?

4. Make a space for this sacred time in your life. When you choose to

show up, it's amazing what you can create. Making the commitment to myself even when I didn't want to or felt like I had nothing to write was life-changing.

These journal exercises do a few things.

1. Create goals of where you'd like to go.
2. Identifies the losses, therefore giving them a voice.
3. Let's tell you the truth, that yes, in fact, something did happen, that you did have feelings about it.

For some, these little steps create a breakthrough. Saying goodbye to the pain is to embrace the freedom that you are not the sum of what you've been through. Does life impact you? YES, of course it does. These things do not define who you are. When we are confused about who we are and whose we are, we live in the identity of what we have survived. I've been sure to add resources at the end to help connect you with the right tools for the process of getting complete when you're ready.

Reflection space:

Seven

Surrendering to the Journey

T here is a process of preparing for creating the life you wish existed. When I was a teenager, I thought it would be so amazing to be an author. I loved how they could take you on a journey and make you a part of it. It felt bigger than what I could accomplish, which was some of the appeal. To imagine something that wasn't real yet. Something to hope for. That someday life serves as an escape for the days when THIS life is a bit too much. My grown-up wish was to share a better way of busting up old belief systems, helping others heal, and inspiring them to claim more for themselves and the people they love. So, I joined the two and wrote this book.

The writing process for this was hard. I am great at talking, but converting conversations into writing was hard. I learned so much in the publishing journey. Albeit, if I had known all that I have learned prior to beginning, I would likely never have done it. Not because of the work, but because there would never have been time for it. Committing to publishing was bold and brave and scary. Especially when my first hurdle showed up. See, you must commit to the end result, and then the journey between where you are and where you want to go becomes solving for the answer (the ending).

When the idea of fulfilling my teenage dreams was first laid on my heart, I heard: "Time to tell the story." I immediately objected, consumed in my own sea of self-doubt, and embarrassed someone would notice. But I was also inspired by the possibility. This is the perfect moment to interject the way I hear God speak in my life.

When people ask: "How do you hear God?" My response is: "When I'm listening." Sometimes, it's through the whisper of a friend. Sometimes, he uses my own voice – I credit Him when I say things I have never thought of before. The words just come out in conversation, making an impact on the moment. Those are inspired words to me. Sometimes it's when I am quiet when I am writing.

Learning to listen *for* Him is such a process—a fairly intense one, at that. I'm learning as we go. I'm committed to the end result of living each day inside of His purpose and brave enough to contribute to this life. To embrace this, I have to be willing to surrender to the journey. And the same is true for you. The more you fight the stirring in your soul, run from it, and negotiate, the harder it is.

When I stopped running, my response to Him was, "You bet! As soon as I figure it out, I will do it." I struggled to overcome the hurdles I perceived would be there if I embraced the journey of publishing a book. The more I thought of the idea of writing, the more I considered **not** writing it. After all, *"Who cares what I have to write?*

The excuses cracked holes in my dreams, like tea in the middle of summer, landing on ice cubes.

"No one would read it anyway."

"I have never written a book."

"I don't know how to publish."

"I don't have the cash flow to be able to fund self-publishing."

on and on….

My pawpaw would say, "It's not *what you think you know*. It's what you *think you know* that *ain't so*. OH, how **THAT** will get you into trouble. All of these objections, and I didn't even know if they were true. They **FELT** true, and it was paralyzing! That's one of the pitfalls of living unaware of the losses that build up over time… We think because things *feel* true, they *are* true. I stated these unknowns as **truths** and felt disempowered, overwhelmed, and so frustrated. I let the fear of the unknown choose for me. I let the version of me I had built to handle loss and grief choose. The version that wants to avoid the pain of rejection because I struggled to see the value in what I had to say.

> "*Most of our dreams, our callings, and the things we want to do but are afraid to follow through with don't see the light of day because we choose to live inside what WE think is possible. We feel the failure of speaking out our dreams only to never see them come to fusion. I cannot impress this more. I hope I am not alone. In my life, I have wanted to succeed so badly (overcoming grief included) I won't try till I have it all figured out. Afraid of looking bad if it takes me longer than I perceive it should. Trapped in the opinion of what I think others think. That's is a dream crusher. Learning to surrender to the journey has been humbling and empowering, like a switch had flipped . I was no longer overcoming struggles. I was solving problems. Committed to my end result.*"

Switching your mindset is something we will discuss in later chapters. For now, I just want you to try to surrender. The process of surrendering your ideas (the things you think you know) about grief, loss, what is possible in relationships, and what you can have in your careers is hard. It's also an easy, quick decision to change. Hard choices can also be easy ones. The part that makes them easy is knowing *WHY*.

When your *WHY* becomes bigger than your *WHY NOT*, you can't help but take action. I cannot decide your *why* for you anymore than you can determine my next move. What I can share with you are some tips.

At the end of chapter 7, I'll give you an exercise to start developing a vision statement for why you want to change and how to surrender to the journey.

As I share this I'll ask you to embrace these three phrases going forward.

- **"Fake it till you make it" is out. *Present* over perfect is in.**
- **Pursue excellence, not perfection.**
- **It's not fun because it's perfect. It's perfect because you made it FUN.**

That last one, it's a bit of a contradiction. I just told you to give up perfection and then I redefined it. Let me explain. My best moments in life, the ones I would choose to stretch a little more in order to savor them longer. In those moments I wasn't chasing perfection. I was having fun. I was present in the moment, standing in it, ready to receive. Giving up perfection is more about let go of the idea we need to ***be*** perfect. Life gets clearer when you embrace the imperfectly perfect MOMENTS.

"I'd rather be 100% present in life with all my imperfections, feeling empowered to contribute to the world; Than to be perfectly faking it in pursuit of making it in this world."

Eight

Accepting and Receiving

⟊ ⟊ ⟊

I t was one of those dreaded, 'Getting to Know you Games.' The ones where you go around the group and offer up a list of trivial things "about" you so everyone can walk away with a few facts and say, "Yeah, I know her." I think the reason I dislike them so much is that they always caused me such anxiety. I felt the need to put my *best foot forward*. Essentially to perform. My pestering desire to also be authentic, accompanied by a desire to please others (insert eye roll), often left me feeling conflicted about what to say. If it was a good day and I shared, I might make someone feel less than or sad. If it was a bad day, I might sound like I'm complaining or ungrateful.

It runs deep in me that I want to be chosen for who I am, not what I do. I assert that so do you. In acknowledging the desire to be fully known and chosen, I discovered a deeply rooted fear. If I was honest about who I was without all the layers of protection, would I be good enough?

If you want to be seen for who you are, you have to tell the truth. So why are we all hiding in plain sight? I found myself at a bit of a crossroads, conflicted about how to change that. I was constantly choosing something pleasing to share, funny to share, or, dare I say, even something not true about myself. Yeah, there were a few times I walked away saying why? Why did you say that?- you don't even like...{whatever it was.} Have you ever done that? Just opened your mouth, and a lie fell out. We call them "little white lies," justifying they don't hurt anyone. Except they do. They hurt you. They show up as layers of filters distorting the real you. Someone once admitted that they are so accustomed to avoiding the pain of loss that they don't even know how things really happen. They have grown so comfortable playing their role. They don't even know what the truth is anymore.

I didn't always live in this conflicted state. I used to be unaware that people don't always choose you for who you are. I thought everyone was good enough. I lived as though I was good enough, unbridled by judgment. Then.

There was a moment that changed all that for me. I remember the first time I didn't feel good enough.

Do you? I bet there was a moment for you too. It was that moment I began to censor myself. ***I decided*** that ***I*** wasn't good enough. I remember thinking I never want anyone to feel the way I feel right now. I was only about nine years old, but it was heart-wrenching. I remember thinking I don't want to be like ***them***. 'Them,' being the people so full of pain. Their pain spills out of them, hurting anyone in the path.

Here's the ugly part of that. We have all made someone, somewhere, feel like they weren't good enough. Intentionally or unintentionally. We are all guilty and all in need of redemption on the matter. That moment shaped much of who I am today, for the good and the bad. At nine years old, I am certain that I didn't see the weight of this moment for anything other than feeling bad. I obviously did not have life figured out OR know that it would still make my heartbeat fast writing it at three decades and some change later. Here's how a moment's like that shape us.

- **EVENT**- what happened
- **YOU REACT**- feelings you have
- **YOU DECIDE**- what you think it means about life and you.
- **YOU CHOOSE**- a coping strategy
- **YOU ACT**- based on the story you created about what happened.

Said another way, something happens, you react to it, then decide what it means about you, build a version of yourself to handle it, to protect you. Most often, we skip the awareness that we can choose whether to build that protective layer, that we have the power to choose, saying, "Even though I am here in this moment with all the pain, I chose NOT to disconnect from it. I choose to embrace it and grow. Instead, we skip this step of awareness and move right to reacting. Want to know the real wild part? We don't even react to what really happened. In the spiral of experiencing grief about what we lost in the moment, we act based on what we "decided" it meant about us. Entangled in a story about who we think we are, we build up walls, finding new ways to protect ourselves. Oh, the ways we try to avoid pain!

The moment you accept responsibility for the power to choose is the moment you become free. I didn't choose until much later in life. Instead, I became a people pleaser. I let my survivor ego drive the getaway car. Out of my pain of rejection and seemingly lack of value, I poured myself into relationships trying to create value. Some people took advantage of that. Others thrived from that. You know what, though? At the end of the day, I was exhausted, trying to make sure everyone felt chosen. As if every unseen heart was the 9-year-old version of me waiting to be good enough.

In that impressionable moment at nine-years-old, I felt disposable and lacking in value. To cope, I created a storyline that if I could really be valuable to someone, they would choose me.

Building value became a theme for me. Disappointing people was uncomfortable. I avoided conflict. Put up with a lot, and boy did I want to save the world.

Hindsight is the best teacher if you view it with *grace*. Many of the themes for my life were born out of some pain I endured, all of these moments shaping me. I spent many years feeling frustrated, confused, and desperate to find my place. If this is you, still wondering where you belong, or worse, realizing that you settled in a role that you don't really like. If you're exhausted trying to right the wrongs, this is for you.

If you are going to find your tribe, you've got to know your vibe.

Sounds cheesy, but how do you know where you fit, If you don't even know who you are? Like most, I had spent a few long years tossing to and fro trying on different versions of myself. Those years led to me feeling unseen, fake-ish, unheard, and a few other things, I'm sure you get the picture. Deciding to accept me was part of the process in shifting my mindset. Acknowledging the grief and loss that had woven its way unseen into my life. I had to be honest with myself and be brave enough to start tearing down the versions I built to protect me from more loss. Start embracing the things that set my soul on fire, regardless if I was the only one. The phrase if you don't stand for something, you'll fall for anything? It's true. I had to learn to stand in who I was, regardless of how messy and imperfect it was. Holding all of who I was and surrendering to the journey of becoming me.

The first time I did this it was at another one of those mixers. I said this time, I want to walk away feeling like they heard me. They know the real me. It was a moment that seemed to go in slow motion. It wasn't earth-shattering news, but the response was shocking. The relief in their eyes almost whispered, how did she just do that. Said what she was actually feeling. Her face matches her feelings. I realized that moment that being authentically flawed- in need of a Savior, was better than faking perfection. Helping others say me too, rather than so what. That. That is the place I wanted to be.

Surrendering to the journey of becoming YOU is an essential step. You have to be willing to embrace the awkwardness of waking your spirit and knowing why you want more. Here's the exercise I promised to get you started.

Discovering WHY and creating a VISION statement.

Thinking about it and doing it are totally different things, but now it's time to make a declaration- A vision statement for the life you want. Really? Just like that? Yep, the idea of a life you love should be free of limits. This is the life you would live if time, money, and resources were unlimited. Are you objecting already? I know it's hard. It was for me too. Trust me. Just do it. The journey to discovering who you are will have plenty of moments for you to retreat to your comfort zone. You'll need to define the "worth it" to keep yourself focused. Developing a vision statement is a great way to do this. As I began to rebuild, I used it as a guide to make choices.

Let's get started:

In examining my life thus far, I felt scattered in *all the things*. I took 3 areas I wanted to continue to spend time in, and I wrote out what my life would look like having achieved success in these areas. I made a conscious decision not to spend time outside of these areas. If I was going to add something new, it needed to align with my vision statement. Establishing a strong vision statement for what will keep you focused on your choices, even in the midst of loss. It will guide you to clarity empowering you to choose an action not based on protecting yourself but in staying aligned with who you are.

* * *

My Vision Statement:

I want to live in a world where people show up for each other. I get to show up for my kids and be with the people who matter when it really matters. I choose people not based on performance but because of love. I no longer tolerate people; I love them. I choose "and" moments that build unity even in adversity. I am willing to stand in the gap, holding the belief that it's possible to create a life you love. I love my career because it is a reflection of all the values I hold dear. I only do the WANT to's, and I said goodbye to the forceful Have to's. I am not obligated. I am motivated. My relationships are a reflection of truth and honesty. People know me because I am not hiding behind a mask, pretending.

Are you objecting again? I know it's hard. We can do hard things. Let's keep going. It is worth noting that a vision statement is deeply personal. It does not have to make sense to anyone else but you. Be sure though, when you say a line, you know exactly what it looks and feels like for YOU. As in, you may not "get" what my vision statement looks like, but I do, which is what's important. When I read it, I have so much clarity that I know exactly what to choose next to honor who I am. Here are some questions to help you begin a vision statement.

1. What do you want?
2. Why do you want it?
3. Why is it important to you?
4. Who wins if you succeed?
5. What is the risk if you don't?

Here is how I answered those questions.

What do you want?

I want to be free.

Why do **you want that?**

I want this life because I believe that it's the best way to live. I believe we were born to be free, not enslaved by fear and the burdens of this world.

Why is it important to you?

I guess I'm bold enough to think I can change the world. Not "I" as in me by myself, but I know the world changes when lots of people do their part. A lot of people doing a little bit will always make an impact. Will it be for good or bad? We will all be accountable for what we contribute in the time we have. I want to be responsible for good stuff. I want to share with others that it is possible. Also that when you are living your best life, you will still have hard days. You will still wonder, am I worthy? That's where the community comes in. A support system of like-minded people ready to whisper your truths back to you when you forget them. Living your best life isn't void of its challenges, but we have subscribed to a lie that everyone else is perfect, and we are the only ones struggling—the Insta life, filter upon filter. We don't extend grace and love. We extend judgment and excuses for not growing.

It's important for me to show people a better way. To stand in the gap for them with the belief that they can create what they wish existed. Then to hand them the tools to accomplish it.

Who wins if you succeed?

Everyone! If I succeed, everyone around me benefits. They benefit when I get to show up for them. My kids see it's possible, and together we have built a community that works together. Everyone benefits *even* if they don't choose to change with me. I benefit because I am free from the burden of opinion. I love people without insisting they perform.

What is the risk if you don't

If I don't find a way to break through, I risk another generation not realizing the freedom that they have if they are brave enough to take action and create what they want. It's important to me I am free to be present with my kids, and when they think of me and my times with them, they remember me being there, not just existing. They see me living life and doing hard things. They see the "worth it."

* * *

RECEIVING

The next step in surrendering to the journey is you've got to be ready to receive. Do you ever struggle with accepting a compliment?

I struggled with the words. You know,...when someone says, "Great job!"... It always made me uncomfortable. I hated taking credit, yet I desired acknowledgment.

No one likes to waste their time. They want to know what they are doing makes a difference. Through my journey with PTA, I have learned what a gift we have to acknowledge and see each other. So many Momma's out there long to be seen, and not in an attention-seeking way. It's just that being a caregiver to tiny humans is often a thankless, exhausting job. It can also be a lonely job. We all have an innate desire to belong and to be a part of something. We also have a desire to be recognized and seen. Unfortunately, somewhere along the line, the natural desire to be seen and recognized gets twisted into a story that you're selfish or attention-seeking if you desire acknowledgment. That perhaps your motives are in the wrong place.

Oh, how I wish we could stop the negative cycle of encouraging people to perform for praise. insisting they must earn the right to be seen, but then shame them into saying things like, "Oh no, it's nothing." Whereby they minimize the impact, they are having on the world. Are you with me? Do you connect with what I'm saying? Learning to receive without shame is not arrogant, lofty, or entitled. Yes, I know there are those people. However, those people aren't the majority. Yet we've course-corrected our lives as if everyone that accepts praise or steps into receiving has questionable motives.

Learning to receive is the other side of a two-headed coin. The other side is giving. Becoming a giver without conditions frees you to accept acknowledgment without shame. One time too many I've heard women downplaying or negotiating a compliment. Wrestling with the shame of saying, "Yeah, that was kinda badass." Instead, we say, "Just doing my job," reducing our value to a bare minimum function that makes the world go round.

I was born a giver. I do not give to get. I love showing up for people and make a continuous effort to work hard and leave anything better than I found it. Yet could I not get to a place of comfort accepting the other side, which is receiving the fruits of my labor. It was all rooted in a philosophy that in order to have pure motives for doing something, you had to do it unseen, **Without recognition.** - this narrative is strong in faith and service communities. It is also a one-way ticket to burn out.

Can you imagine living with that thought process? It's exhausting. You end up dodging every compliment and downplaying your efforts. "No big deal, I just made a little costume," All the while, knowing how much work you did invest. The subconscious is a beast and left untamed. You go on autopilot. Before you know it, it's 'just the way you are.' The long-term impact of that kind of thinking was I began dialing back what I was capable of. Afraid someone would notice. If I was too big, I might overshadow someone else. Oh, what a tangled web we weave.

Through the journey of learning to receive, I was able to accept and embrace this statement. "You are extraordinary," going from negotiating compliments to embracing that I was extraordinary took a Brave Heart. I had to embrace that I am extraordinary not by the world's standards, but embracing I was extraordinary by the GRACE of God. I am a reflection of His mercies and work. Receiving the acknowledgment is accepting that today the world got to experience God. He used me to show up in the world and they noticed, even if they didn't acknowledge it was Him.

I started out small. Just saying, "Thank you for noticing." I also had to accept that my purpose was to create little moments each day in the world where God was showing up. To give my very best and let Him do the rest. It wasn't ME that was receiving praise. It was Him. He is the giver of all my talents. When I use them, I am honoring the time He took to develop me. Receiving the compliment, the fruits of that manifestation, is just the other side of the giving coin. Neither can know their value without each other. Be a giver, THEN be ready to receive.

Wash. Rinse. Repeat.

The gift I get to give others is to tell them how extraordinary they are by the grace of God and how it's time they let Him take credit for it. Stop negotiating your value and what you are comfortable with. Letting their light shine is SHOWING the world how good God is, not how good you are.

Embrace that...

Nine

Embrace Your Brave Heart

*f you're still reading this, you'll know my Brave Heart is at the heart of the approach. I've used the word embrace and words like surrender and rise to describe moving through life. You may be saying, what is a Brave Heart? What does it look like? Do I have one? Why Raising Brave Hearts? Let me explain.

Brave Hearts is a moment. Raising them is how we do it.

* * *

Embracing your Brave Heart is A defining moment we come to where we are free from the pain of the past, free to live FULLY in the moment, even when it's painful.
We are hopeful for the future.

The last step of surrendering to the journey of becoming you is the beginning of what comes next. As I reflected on how to pull this book together, what to include, and what to leave out. It came to me as I learned another lesson. I'd like to share that story with you. It's from my journal where I was writing about feeling a bit too much.

Journal entry

It has been a rough few days. My sweet friend has a beautiful place outside of town. She is so generous with her care of others. She had said if I need some alone time to feel free to come out. The graciousness of her offer was not wasted. I asked if she could make space for me today because today was laundry day.

It was getting noisy and messy in my mind. I have been stepping over all the words and thoughts like piles of dirty laundry and avoiding them in the same way. I packed my earbuds to drown out the noise and fully intended on floating in the pool listening to tunes, but God had other plans. He whispered, "today, you need to hear all the words—no more stepping over them or shoving them in a basket, hiding them in the closet. Today you need to hear all of them. Today you need to leave it in the water."

So today, I did my laundry in my friend's pool.

Gather. Sort. Wash. Dry. Fold and put them where they belong. I felt a whisper of the word {restore} then this:
"These thoughts you've been having, the words floating around. They don't belong on the floor or stuffed in a basket. They have a purpose. Restore them to their proper place."

Some of my thoughts required a gentle cycle. Some were heavily soiled; some were bulky and needed an extra spin cycle. But it all came out in the wash.

Let's give this some context before you go too far down the path of me literally washing my clothing in my friend's pool.

* * *

I have made it a practice to take things to the water, to wash them in God's grace, before presenting them to the world. I pray he will wash my words, that he will cover them in his Grace and bring them out clean again. I just love how He modeled these processes for us. If we would just embrace them, we could spend our lives *doing* rather than *figuring out*.

I'm offering you a moment of connection. We all have our gifts. One of mine is to notice connections and give them a voice. Making hard things user-friendly.

See, I had been searching for a word to describe a process of what raising Brave Hearts meant. This section wasn't always called EMBRACE, although I had used the word embrace several times already. It was literally hiding in plain sight. Ever have a solution hidden in plain sight?

I acknowledge that it's been a struggle to get there. I think most of the book was written before I came back and added this in. I tried using different words to describe the moment we need our Brave Hearts. Complete. Present. Aware. While they do have a place in the journey, they just didn't fit for me. There was also this word {overcome} that was bothering me. It kept popping up, and I didn't like it.

When I hear overcome, it feels like a struggle. Brave hearts don't struggle. I am not saying they don't have hard things to do in life. I'm saying they don't wrestle in the mud with their hard times. They don't choose to stay in the mess, finding new ways to rehash it. **They don't** make things hard. They embrace the hard things. Standing in the moment as it is, ready for what's next.

Raising Brave Hearts in ourselves and each other is about practicing the moment of EMBRACE, then rising. The day I went to the pool, the 'too much" I had been wrestling with was some of the things I had to write about. If there was too much "Jesus" for the world? There I said it.

46

I'm embarrassed that I would even think about it, but I find myself tailoring my words to avoid pushing anyone away. Writing for the world, not for God.

* * *

Journal entry continued:

I could hear the cycle of the filter, the trickle of the water flowing through. I'm sorry, please forgive me. I wasn't listening to you. I'm listening now. What's the word? {EMBRACE}

I furrowed my brow. It was like I was standing over the word, examining it from all angles. What does it mean? Can I use it here? What does it feel like? I went for my phone. Googled - "definition of embrace" WOWZA!

{EMBRACE}

To take up especially ready or gladly.

To avail oneself of: embrace the opportunity to study further.

To take in or include as a part of a more inclusive whole

{EMBRACE} is definitely the perfect word to describe a Brave Heart;

Are you ready for another story? Here's what {Embrace} looks like in action.

Floating in the pool was the revealing of a word I've already been living. My journals were full of this word, yet it's as if I was completely unaware of how powerful it was until I started trying to explain Brave Hearts.

I saw this meme early in 2020 that said, "Whoever was supposed to go to Nineveh... go already." I saw it a bunch, so many times, I began to think maybe I was meant to pay attention. The first time I laughed. Next, I scrolled by. Next time I got annoyed. Then as fortune would have it, it was used in a sermon at church. THEN, it hit me! What if it was me? And it was YOU, and WE were supposed to go.

2020 seemed the first six months of the year were tearing down, constant reflection, and many questions of "WHY?" Why is this happening? Before you go there, let me pull you back to what I am saying. I am not saying I caused the pandemic or the world is waiting on me. I am not asserting that I AM that significant. I am suggesting, what if…*we all are.*

See, I figure if it's true for me, it's probably true for some of you. I've been hiding, hushing the voice, the nudges, and the nuances in how I see God in the world. Have you? Is that too big? Are my problems too big for God? Are my dreams too big? I've been there, some days I am there. What would the world look like IF all the believers stood up and said, It was me, I was supposed to go to Nineveh.

They stopped hiding and hushing the Holy Spirit and acknowledged the power of the WHAT IF … There is power in that statement and freedom to look at your life and take action as IF it were true. We are entangled in needing facts and need to feel valued to answer the call. To feel worthy.

So, What if it? What if it was you? What if YOU stood up and said, It was me, I was supposed to go to Nineveh? What if you Repented and EMBRACED what the Holy Spirit places on your heart? You repented for hiding from the way you felt called to love the LORD. My friend Joann says when you don't love God the way you were designed to, He misses that. NO one can love God the way you do.

Ok, I have a big ask. I need you PAUSE and hold that Idea of you embracing what you feel called to do, and then add this bit in.

My son lied to me this week. When I discovered this, I was crushed. In our chat about truth, trust, and forgiveness, he said. "If I were you, I would never trust anyone again." I gently said, well, that would be a sad life. Jesus asks us to forgive. If we didn't forgive, we wouldn't be able to restore what was broken. Life is about choosing together. I can't change or fix what was broken {the trust}, but I can choose forgiveness, and through that, we can restore. I choose together, what do you want to choose?

Our great moments in life are when we stand and say, IT WAS ME!

We accept responsibility, then we kneel and say forgive me for hiding, we EMBRACE forgiveness and choose to live in the power of being restored.

"Isaiah 43:19 and it says
" See, I am creating a new thing. Now it springs up, do you not perceive it? I am
making a way in the wilderness and streams in the wasteland."

What if it was you, it was your dream, your vision, YOU the world is waiting on to come out of hiding, to RISE and embrace courage and vulnerability.

Surrendering to the journey of raising your Brave Heart, being open to receiving it,
and embracing what life would look like having achieved it, is the beginning of
your Brave Heart rising. It's the beginning of waking your spirit.

You're alive because of your heart. You're LIVING when you find
a way to follow it.

Reflection space:

III

Part Three

It's a risky business, full out kinda living.
Some may argue a life reserved for the carefree or perhaps the
more widely recognized extrovert.
Introverts or extroverts, the shared truth is we all have feelings.
You are either embracing your feelings or struggling against them.

Ten

It's Time for Rising

ndated Journal entry:
  …Why are we all so different, yet recognize so much in each other?
  I think we recognize pain, and we recognize love—two sides of a coin.
The more I live, the more I believe it boils down to a simple matter of BIG LOVE.
Learning to live in love, not just speak truth, but to live truth in love.

Consider for a moment, if you will, healing our hearts is not enough. We were not meant to take possession of our struggles and to overcome them. We were meant to rise and be resurrected from them. Much like Lazarus in the bible, Jesus could heal him from afar, but He didn't. It wasn't a question of could he heal. If you will permit me the liberty, I believe we can consider the possibility the emphasis on healing wasn't enough. He didn't want Lazarus to be healed from his pain but to be completely raised from it. To be newly restored.

We see this concept of completing the old life and raising a new life play out in scripture all the time, including Jesus' own resurrection story. It was necessary and essential for him to not only heal from his wounds but to die completely. EVERYTHING was left nailed to the cross. To rise out of the pain, not just to overcome it.

I have a conflict in teaching a method as a specialist and knowing my Savior's power. Often there is a social influence to separate them. To pick which to follow. Telling Christians if they don't *just* use God, then it's because their faith is weak and telling people who use a process they need to keep God out of it so that everyone will use it. I stand for the power of AND moments. When society says pick one, you say no thanks. I'll have both.

I have found embracing the gap of God's and what's mine is using a process to take action in my life. A process that has helped me understand His grace, forgiveness, and restoration more than ever before. I understand His gift of *free will* came at such a price. He was willing to say, even if you don't come back to me, I don't want you to live as a product of what happens in this fallen world. I want you to choose, to have the ability to create a meaningful life. I am in awe of the responsibility this freedom calls us to. I am grateful, and I don't want to waste it.

Today the trend is striving to be better versions of ourselves. Yes, I agree. I also believe the best version of you is less about your personality, MORE about what God can do through you. Less about where you are. More about where God wants to lead you.

Less can be More when the less *of you is embracing* MORE *of him.*

In that moment, I believe you ARE fulfilling your purpose. Anytime you are letting him do the leading, you're serving and allowing him to fill you. YOU are walking in His purpose for YOUR life. This awareness stopped my search for the answer to "what's my purpose?" We are the fingerprints of God and the reflection of all the many ways HE touches lives. It feels good to be emptied at the work of serving the Lord. It can be as ordinary as a cup of cool water or as tedious as launching a new ministry. It may be as meaningful as checking on a friend who is grieving or, dare I say, as difficult as responding kindly with patience to a child who has asked the same question six ways from Sunday.

Walking in the purpose of being His hands and feet is only possible when we stop trying to separate our lives on earth from our life with Him. It's more than a Sunday morning to-do list.

Learning the skills to live complete and free of the burden from unfinished business in the past, learning to forgive the unforgivable, and let go of the pain is what we are called to do as followers of Christ. It was work, and I needed the steps to break it down to take action. Introvert or extrovert feeling fulfilled like you have a purpose is a deep and appropriate desire. Giving a voice to your purpose is the hard part. Getting complete with the grief which stands in the way is part of revealing the voice inside you.

Reflection space:

Eleven

Making Space

"A Brave Heart is grateful for all the moments"

The moments consumed me.
I couldn't breathe. I was hanging on to everything,
afraid to lose more.

Journaling has taught me a discipline that really connected in the moments I sat by my father's bed as he was nearing his final days. Another one of those messy moments in life where you don't know whether to hang on for dear life or let go and just be. As I sat there beside him collecting memories afraid, I wouldn't remember, it clicked! I needed to release it. I needed to get it out so I could allow more in.

You're biologically designed to avoid pain. Emotional and physical. It's part of our survival instinct.

Every workshop I lead has a section dedicated to identifying loss. It's powerful - like a veil lifting. When you realize grief is our emotional reaction to loss and loss is always walking next to us, you begin to see the daily impact all around you of people living with cumulative incomplete loss.

Some loss shows up as invisible as the loss of hopes, dreams, or expectations. These intangible losses are tough. You can't put your finger on an event. However, you can most definitely see and feel the impact of them in your life. These show up as feelings of burn out, frustrations, anger—Times of sadness in your life. Feeling like you've lost your joy, or you are just going through the motions. NOTE: I am not a psychiatrist. I am not diagnosing NOR recommending you stop medication. I am suggesting if you recognize these feelings, you give yourself a break and stop being so hard on yourself, asking WHAT IS WRONG with me. Nothing is wrong.

You are grieving. You may not know what you are grieving, but you are emotionally responding to loss. Situational depression is not the same as being clinically depressed. When dad died, I found myself at a loss. Quite literally, but I didn't know the loss of my dad in death and the loss of expectations were separate. I just lumped them into one "I feel broken" comment. I felt like I should know what to do. After all, I did have a degree in psychology. I was well-read. I should know how to deal with this…right? I mean, if you can't deal with it intellectually, there is always your faith… right? The way you survive, it is just to have bigger faith…right?

This "I need to do more" mentality really let me down. I traded my heart for a how-to manual and tried to intellectualize my grief. It contributed to me feeling like something was wrong with ME. In search of a solution, I went to a weekend retreat for grievers. It's where my journey as a specialist began. I learned I wasn't broke, just my tools. It was eye-opening to me, and in my healing was born a deep desire to give access to this success to others.

These are my heart's desires to open a world you once wished for and have now created. Moving from wishing to creating; To cheer and guide you into the most fulfilling chapter of your life.

YOU the ones saying YES to this. You are my people. And my tribe. In order to do this, we have to embrace the idea- if your heart is full of yesterday's moments, you won't be able to receive today's gift. Today is its own space in the world. We must embrace living present and on purpose. Be willing to acknowledge the hard stuff, do the work, and rising from it, complete with gratitude, having gained those experiences.

I know I share much of my dad's death when I speak to my experience with grief and loss. The impact of his death was my birth to grief awareness and the role loss plays in shaping our actions. It helped me see so many other areas of life I did not realize I have been grieving. In examining this concept of grief transcending to other areas of life outside death, I discovered a whole world of loss I had been avoiding. Before you start panicking for me, let me remind you. It's only our lack of tools that create the unwillingness to explore enlightenment.

Think about your car. The change oil light comes on. If you don't know how to change the oil, you take it to the shop. If you know the basics, you might attempt on your own, but ask for help from someone who knows more. A third scenario might be you feel confident in your ability to handle the situation. However, you get into the oil change and discover a broken tool and learn you will have to get new tools before you can finish. The very worst thing you can do is ignore the change oil light. It is going to cause infinite damage down the road and involuntarily stop you in your tracks. The long-term impact of an unresolved oil change can be very expensive. You can't just maintain oil by continuing to top it off, mixing the new with the old. That filter needs to be changed, and the old oil flushed out. It's served its purpose and is no longer benefiting your vehicle. It needs to be changed for a reason. Completely cleaned out and renewed is how your vehicle was designed to work. We don't argue with this because it's logical. We know these facts to be true, and bonus, our vehicles are equipped with a light to alert us when this change needs to occur. Wouldn't it be lovely if we were provided with such a light? DING DING, time to exchange those old ideas and coping strategies. They are no longer benefiting you!

* * *

In retrospect, I was our friend. I was the friend ignoring the oil change continuing to dump quarts of oil into the car.

"Because I "didn't have time."

"Didn't want to open that can of worms."

"It is what it is."

"That's what happens in business.

"Suck it up, buttercup."

I bought into the *"It doesn't matter how many times you fall, just how many times you get back up."* That phrase appealed to my survivor ego. Just get back up. So, I did. I got up and took all my stuff with me each time. I dealt with the unexpected events in my life by trying to maintain life. As long as I could just get back up, everything would be ok. Forget thriving. I just wanted to survive.

Incidentally, I would not describe myself as controlling. In fact, if you know me, you'd likely agree. You might even think I am easy going and flexible. I found I could only be this way in my comfort zone. I am only easy going when all my pillars are stable. **Faith, Family, and Finance.**

Take out one of those; Me avoiding God's requests, my dad dying, my business tanking. You might as well pop the popcorn and watch the unraveling. When one of those gets affected, the only logical response is to sound the alarm and hunker down for the storm. Right?

Are you ready for my epic coping strategy? If you guessed my strategy for dealing with loss was to avoid more loss, you'd be right. Controlling the chaos. If I could just hold the line and not lose any more ground. Avoid more loss. It would be enough.

Maintaining life is an insane thought in hindsight. It's impossible to maintain something that's always changing. Desperately trying to keep things the same even though they were forever different. I retreated to a comfort zone painted with an illusion of safety.

From this place of safety, I could manage everything. I took very limited risk. I was settled and felt safe. Then one day or a series of days, I realized by not risking, I'm not living. I had allowed myself to grow stale and was feeling empty. I was knowingly choosing not to pursue my dreams because I didn't want to lose anything else. The Salt in the wound is I believed I deserved a break from working hard at life. I became entitled to settling.

I managed to twist this scenario, where I started to act like it was ok to not live life to the fullest. Not fulfill your potential. Like I deserved to be ok for a while. "<u>OK!</u>"

"Ok" is harder work in the long run because it requires you to silence the stirring. If you've ever tried to hush a crying baby in church, this is where I was when I decided to stop trying to make decisions based on what I thought I deserved. To shift to a state of gratitude for how these events will help me grow. Here this. Gratitude can also be sad. I didn't magically take a happy pill, and everything was hunky-dory. Practicing gratitude allows you to shift into a momentum of solving and creating. Looking forward, rather than stubbornly digging your heels in, saying, I don't deserve this. This shift is what allows you to begin making space for healing and creating.

Reflect and Grow

Pick an area of life you want to improve; that you wish was different. Journal about how you are grateful for the moment you are in. You are alive, have free will, and have the power to take actions today that will change your tomorrow. Unlock this entitlement by taking responsibility for what comes next.

Before you get started, I'll share this. My son came walking into the living room, sleepily one morning. "Mooommmmm," he moaned. "My legs hurt."

He and a friend had been competing with a new workout challenge. Landon is active and healthy. My point is even though you think you're doing all the right things when you try on a new skill you haven't tried or done in a long time, you'll feel it. Keep working to strengthen these muscles of emotional resilience. I promise it's worth it.

* * *

Here's an outline to get you started on a gratitude mindset. You may even find some areas of loss surface. That's ok. Use this to get you started in your journaling.

- Today I am grateful for:
- Today I expected:
- Today these are the things I wish were better, more or different:
- Today I forgive:

Reflection space

Twelve

Forgiving

~~~~~~~~~~~~

"A Brave Heart knows how to forgive."

I hear it all the time. "Why is it so hard to forgive?" It's the easiest, hardest question I've ever answered. It's hard to forgive because we aren't loving. First, Corinthians in the bible is one of the most beautiful descriptions of love. We have reduced it to a nice scripture to read at weddings as if the only kind of love is romantic.

Love and forgiveness are partners. They exist together. Social influences say forgiving is forgetting and love is love. Wait. How can you love someone yet still keep a record of their wrongs? The best version of love is when you can love someone without insisting they please you. Loving yourself is growing to a place where you can acknowledge other people and their opinions but still choose what aligns with you. Free from others' opinions but still very much engaged in how others think and feel about life. Let's break this down a bit.

Loving without a record of wrong:

I used to think this was forgetting, and then I read a quote somewhere. It's not that you don't forget. It's that you forgive. That part made sense. BUT how do you forgive without forgetting? I spent years living what I thought was forgiveness, only to be humbled learning it truly was not.

I walked into a room one day and saw someone who has caused me great pain in my life. I saw them standing there and, for the most part, had repeatedly patted myself on the back for being the bigger person, by which I should allow them the privilege of still being part of my life. I was justified in my pain. I deserved never to forget. Do you have someone like that? A person you've had to be the bigger person and tolerate them. Love them where they are at? You might even want to argue if I only knew I'd understand!

The moment I saw them, the judgment poured out of me. Examining all the ways in which they were failing in life, all the annoyances buzzed over me like a swarm of mosquitos. All the ways in which I would change them if they would get their act together. I know. It's ok to judge me. I did. Then seemingly out of nowhere, in the midst of my self-righteous moment. "This is not love" washed over me. "This is not grace" "Have I not forgiven you for your judgmental heart" I had this flash of the endgame.

You know the moment you stand accountable for your life. The one question He asks me is, "Why didn't you LOVE the unlovable." In that moment, years of pain poured out of my eyes. I was the one who needed forgiveness.

Forgiveness is not keeping a record. It's loving someone. Period. I have always been so sensitive to people saying, "I love them where they are at." No, you don't. That's keeping a record. It's not love. I can hear you now; "Well, you know what I mean. I'm not going to try to change them. I love them despite themselves." NOPE, still keeping a record. If you truly love someone, you love them for the whole and complete person, GOD, designed them to be. Not for who they show up as from time to time; the imperfectly, wounded, and less than version of themselves. You love them so much you don't measure their progress. You don't say things like, "I see you growing." YOU just love them so big they have so much room to be who God intended for them. NONE of us are whole and complete.

We have all got things we do and naturally cannot see because those are our things. If someone has told you, they love you *inspite* all your screw ups.

Know this, God loves you and sees all of you. He designed you and created you whole and complete lacking in nothing. Our journey here on earth leaves battle wounds. Those wounds do not define the LOVE we are called to receive or to give. Love keeps no record of wrong. It is whole and complete. It is big and bold and defies what we deserve. Give it anyway. Love others. Love yourself.

Loving yourself means you have to forgive yourself too. Acknowledge the wrongs, embrace the freedom of forgiveness, and LOVE.

Thirteen

The Table

We are a *show-up* family, even when things are bad. When your flaws are bigger than you think people can handle. It's been hard to keep coming to the table each year. We've had our share of lifetime movie moments, drama, deception, pain, shame and regret. We've also experienced some great hallmark movie moments of peace, redemption, healing, and forgiveness. We choose together. Do what you have to do to get back to the table. The world is designed to push us apart. Filling our lives with justification for quitting on each other.

Creating a life you love is also about being with the people you *LOVE*. Discovering the path to completing wounded relationships and choosing the way back to the table is a huge part. You can want all the things for your life and BIG dreams, but what does it matter if you have lost so many relationships in the process?

One of the greatest gifts we can give each other is forgiveness. As a family growing up, we always ate at the dinner table. We all went our separate ways through the day, but the symbolism of gathering together again at the end of the day was deeply rooted. One of those principle lessons you have no idea you're learning, especially on those nights where everyone is fighting, when it's hard to stay together. Here's the thing, when we are all struggling to stay together is exactly when we need to stay together. Please don't misunderstand this example. There were many years after we were all grown and had moved into our own lives with our own tables to fill at the end of the day, it was really hard to make coming back to "our" table together a priority. There were empty seats, some unwillingly left empty, like when Dad died. Some on purpose, because someone chose to leave.

It would have been easy to quit choosing each other. To move on with our lives and accidentally see each other once in a while. To vow to just do a better job with our own families - it would have been a mistake. I want to live a life committed to doing the work to get back to the table with the people I love. In the process, I don't want to lose sight of The Ultimate Table. Our Heavenly Father's table. Each of us has our lives to live here on earth, our own business to tend to, our purpose to fulfill. We must do whatever it takes to get back to the ultimate table and make sure when you look around. You see the people you love, recognize the soul of the people you did life with, and say, because of Christ living through you, I can sit here.

Forgiveness is key to getting back to the table.

My kids bless them. They say I'm sorry, at least 2-3 times a day. This is a new phase for us as they experiment with this self-regulating phase in which they explode and then reel it back in. Learning how to "make it right" with each other is something I want to instill in them. I model taking responsibility for what comes next. Initiating coming back together as often as possible. To see them begin to take ownership of this has my heart beaming. When they started this "I'm sorry," I wanted to be sure they heard and learned to say "I FORGIVE YOU" Then I found myself saying I forgive you, I forgive you, I forgive you. While YES, I forgive you is the appropriate response; it felt like something was missing in the intentionality of what I wanted them to learn. Forgiveness is a word we struggle to understand. I mean, we've already bought into the lie 'forgiving is forgetting' and if we've experienced pain, we hold out on forgiveness as a way of protecting ourselves from experiencing more loss. Forgiveness is a completion moment. It says I choose to love you.

Love keeps no record of wrongs, and it doesn't treat you like you failed.

I wondered how I could start responding to help them learn through the experience and have more words.

This is how I chose to respond. Stop, turn, make eye contact.

"Thank you for acknowledging that happened and taking responsibility for making it right. I forgive you, and I love you. Now that we have it down, I look at them and say, "Thanks for taking responsibility, thanks for showing up on that one."

Gratitude goes with forgiveness in the same way it goes with love. At the very least, forgiving someone is YOU taking responsibility for choosing LOVE. I'm doing my part to raise Brave Hearts who know HOW to apologize AND how to forgive. I know not every injustice has someone on the other end just waiting to tell you I'm sorry for hurting you. The beautiful part of forgiveness. You can forgive even when they don't know they need forgiving. It belongs to all of us, and none of us are free from the responsibility of choosing to come back to the table.

Reflections

I wanted to share this journal moment with you. It was a time full of many emotions, and it deserves its place in this book. Relationships are incredibly important to me. We are built for connection and live in a world which is decidedly trying to separate us from each other. Our best lives are when we find a way back to the table; The Ultimate Table, The Lord's Table, and we do it together. In order to accomplish this, we have to 'LET IT GO.' Choose the person instead of the flaws. But, like many things, life itself has been faithful at standing in the way of taking action, and for a long time, I had been willing to let it.

Journal Entry

"I'm not going to lie; things have been better. A lot's going on, not sure how it will all work out, but I am just feeling defeated. I have a great sense of loss, and I am trying to figure out how I can block it out or not

let it bother me. I mean, I know how I am. I tend to give more than I have and end up short-changed by people. It's definitely hard to find a balance. I'm really angrier than anything, and I feel trapped. I don't know what else to say. I wish things were different...I wish we still talked. I wish a lot of things were different, and I wish I could come to a peace within and just let go of what was and try to make a better future."

I had tried many times to restore this broken relationship. The brokenness between my sister and me. In the moments of that journal entry, the memories of the joy we once shared left me yearning for a time of restoration. The cycle of forgiving each other through the years went a little like this.

Explosive fight, silence, need each other again, exchange apologies, time of peace, one misspoken word, then the rush of ALL past indiscretions, surges of emotion, entitled statements "She's always like this" "When will I learn, she'll never change" "She thinks she's better than everyone" The list went on. Pause for a moment and jot down some statements you say about your person when your hurt.

We lived in this cycle of pain, never allowing each other any room to be anything other than our worst parts. Like we'd created wrap sheets for each other. The prison sentence kept growing for each repeat offense. We had imprisoned each other with a life sentence, and a heaping dose of that's as good as it gets. Occasionally letting one another out for good behavior only to double the sentence at the mere hint of not measuring up to expectations. There was no room for grace. It was self-preservation and pride standing in the way of choosing each other. I wish I could say this relationship was the only relationship I have ever taken a measuring stick to. It's not.

Tensions were high. It was our first visit with each other since sobriety became part of her story. I was rushing to get ready in the morning.

NOTE:-DO NOT *try to have a restorative conversation on a timeline. It will not work.*

She appeared in the doorway, "Hey, I've been wanting to say something to you. I feel like you haven't really forgiven me. Like you still only see the version of me that makes mistakes. I was just wondering if you had plans to really ever forgive me."

A thousand daggers would have been less painful in that moment-what I have learned over and over again is pain will make you say stupid things. Fear of loss will entice trauma driven fight or flight responses EVERY. TIME.

The boiling inside me caused my jaw to clench. I tried to busy myself with the next makeup tool, trying to make space and time for my response.

"So, are you?" she coaxed. It felt like a test. It was a test.

"You know what," I jeered- not even taking my eyes off my reflection in the mirror as I studied and admired my well-applied make-up.

"If you weren't so focused on trying to prove to everyone how much you've changed, maybe some of us could begin to trust you again. You just need to give me time to see if this is the new you."

If I could go back to that moment, I would have dropped my makeup and embraced her with all those years of pain between us. I would have said I forgive you.

I missed that moment with her. Instead, she retreated to her space in the world I had made for her in my mind. She settled into playing her role as my screw up little sister, committed to always trying, never quite getting there.

The years passed, and we both enjoyed the break from our cycle of abusing each other with our words. We learned how to be civil and work together, even to enjoy each other. We tried just to move on. I mean, how do you unpack a relationship of pain? How do you restore the broken hopes and dreams you had? Isn't it enough we just don't fight? We grew into tolerating each other. It would have been a stretch to say what we had was a loving relationship, at least in the way I understand love now.

I went to a retreat once to grow my business skills. I *love* how we pick something to blame for why we aren't achieving our goals be it relationship goals or personal goals. For me, I want to create a breakthrough in self-limiting beliefs in business. I could not have been more misguided in thinking why I was there. I was there to learn how to let go.

The exercise for the break was powerful. The assignment was to choose someone to love because YOU choose them. To take responsibility for what you have done in the relationship, without any conditions attached. To stand in a place of letting go. The objective was to create moments of personal power. To notice you have the right to choose a different life at any moment.

I knew *she* was my person. All I could see was her phone number. I called three other people to forgive, receiving voicemail after voice mail. I took a bathroom break and tried to let myself off the hook with a "Good enough try" pat on the back. Then there was this.

"I thought you wanted to create a life you wish existed. Who is with you in the life you create? Do you really love Or do you tolerate people, hoping someday they will change? Whose responsibility is it to complete the pain you have?"

ME! All fingers pointed to me. I ruffled for my phone, simultaneously searching for a clock to check the time. Maybe there wasn't enough time to fix this one. Maybe I should just take this intention and sort it out later. Maybe it's too late, she's probably busy, but maybe instead I'll just tell her a little about the breakthrough SHE can have at one of these weekends... my mind raced with all the ideas of what I would say.

"Hello," A moment as wide as the Grand Canyon spilled into the space between Hello and what came next.

"I'm sorry I haven't been loving you. All this time, I have been pretending I forgive you, when in fact, I have just been keeping score. I have been so afraid of getting hurt, afraid of losing more, I just drew a box around how big I thought we could love each other and forced myself to be ok with it. I am not. When I look at my life, I want to choose people for who they were made to be and for all that is possible for them. I want to be loved for who I am, beyond the flaws that show up sometimes. I want to be chosen for who I am. I don't want to spend any more time tolerating myself or the people in my life. I have been unfair to you. Limited your growth in my mind and loved you where you are. I want to create a relationship with you based on choosing each other, loving, dreaming, and creating together. Will you stand with me in what we can be?" Silence.

"Please, Lord. Don't let me reap what I've sown."

"Are you there?"

"I haven't really been loving you either." Her voice came back, competing with the emotion of the moment. "I forgive you." We both held space to cry. When I dialed her number I received more than a phone connection. Miles apart and yet closer than ever.

"Ok! I have to go. Thank you for choosing us with me. I love you and can't wait to see you."

YEARS of pain completed in less than two minutes. Two minutes of honesty and personal responsibility has gifted us both a relationship you would never have imagined was possible given the pain we shared.

This is forgiveness. We have had plenty of opportunities to tolerate each other in the years following our moments of truth, and sometimes we did. Sometimes we showed up for each other as *less than* versions of our true selves, making it difficult to love each other. In those moments, we had to stop, choose open and honest. Choose forgiveness again. Choose each other again. We had to keep growing and loving. We had to embrace grace. Forgiveness is not something you only do once. It is something you do all the time. You keep choosing LOVE.

* * *

I want you to explore what forgiveness and love look like in your own relationships. If you didn't pick someone earlier to write out some limiting statements. Pick someone now.

Don't pick the second person who comes to mind. Pick the first person you think of when you say:

"The person I need to forgive is _____*."*

Take your person and write out what you've wished your relationship was like.

Next, write all the things they have done to you, and how you feel about it.
You now have where you are and where you want to be.
The journey 'between' begins with forgiveness.

Take the list of wrongs and begin to re-write this statement. *"I forgive you for the time you (insert event)."*

Do this for each painful experience. It's important you feel supported to interchange the following phrase.
"I acknowledge what you did, and I choose not to allow the pain to stop me from loving you any longer."

Sometimes it more appropriate to embrace YOU are choosing forgiveness for you, not them. You are choosing, even if they don't acknowledge the pain you feel. You are the only person who can choose to see right past all the imperfection and love who they are; The version of themselves before they too put on all the layers of protection.

THIS IS IMPORTANT. This letter of sorts is for YOU. I knew my sister was a safe place to say this out loud. Most of what I had to say to her was ME taking responsibility.

I do not recommend going to every person you want to forgive and announcing you forgive them. The moment you decide to forgive happens instantaneously. Living in forgiveness and loving others is a daily action.

There are many days my sister and I had to remind ourselves we *"Already forgave that." "We already said goodbye to that pain."* You can do this too. You must stand in the commitment to yourself saying

I forgive, and I CHOOSE love.

Fourteen

Might be Smiling, But I'm Lying

s I stared at the picture of me, I noticed it didn't match the reality. It was an ah-ha moment, but I had no idea how to fix it. I felt sad. I thought to myself, why spend all your time on something you aren't really living or loving. It's the complete opposite of who I wanted to be. That moment of awareness felt lonely and overwhelming.

God has blessed me with many gifts. I want to use them, ALL of them. The problem is I was trying to do EVERYTHING myself. My life resembled a one-act play; I was doing quick costume changes, being This to them and That to "it." I felt tired. I had the longest-running act on Broadway. {See what I did there} This is your money well spent! I need you to hear me! I WAS NOT BEING FAKE! Except I was. I really did mean everything I did. I meant it when I showed up to things, I was involved because I wanted to, but I was performing at all these roles. If I can do all these things well enough, If I work hard enough, If I show up enough, Then I will be enough. When you live like that, your gift often becomes your joy stealer.

Sure, I intellectually knew you couldn't derive value from doing things, in the same way, you can't "earn" salvation, yet here we are, most of us living to EARN something. A promotion, A paycheck… We perform in our relationships; we are set up socially to earn the title of good enough. We have compartmentalized life and said, now go be good at all of it.

The lie of having it all together is it starts with stuff you really like to do anyway, so it's easy at first- that's when you get hooked. Everyone loves to win- so you do what you have to so you can keep winning. The LIE:

> *EVEN when you're losing, FIND a way to look like you're still winning.*
> *Performing in your life, so you don't have to own the grief attached to*
> *the loss of the unmet expectations, the things we wished for that never*
> *came to be.*

You'll know you're losing when your face stops matching the feelings. When your smile is there, but your eyes don't sparkle. When you decide to be so strong for others, you become weak. When you stay so busy, you miss out on cups of tea with your little one which undoubtedly has more than "1 lump or 2" of sugar in it.

If you said, "Me too" you get it. Life is lonely when you feel like you are the only one "not winning." When you are caught up in the performances and the Insta- life filter. Our focus shouldn't be who has the best performance.

The focus should be; living authentically, bravely, and intentionally in a way which helps others find *Me too moments,* so they don't feel alone.

So, what did I do? I alluded to this decision I made in the previous chapter, where I was confronted with the moment to delay forgiveness with my sister. This is how the decision to change came to be. The decision to begin creating the life I had been wishing existed.

After crying a lot and moping for a few days, maybe months, it's all a bit of a blur. I decided to stop lying to myself and everyone around me. I mean, it wasn't like I was lying in the traditional understanding of the phrase. Lie to avoid punishment or to manipulate. I was trying to avoid pain—the pain of not being good enough.

* * *

What if I stop *doing*... what will happen?

In the banking world, it's called kiting. The term basically means if you stop doing what you're doing to make everything look good, it reveals a really big mess. If you do this in banking, you go to jail. Do it in your job, and you'll likely get fired. The consequences of kiting your life are sometimes never fully realized until much, much later. "Fake it till you make it" is a popular phrase, but it's a lie and a joy stealer. "Present over perfect" is a choice and, while hard, is much more rewarding. I'd rather live a life aware of its imperfections and be able to own them and draw strength from them than to spend all my energy trying to overcome them…to outperform them, or worse. Pretend they don't exist.

Learning to live presently was a beginning step for me. The best advice I received was when my dad was in his final stages.

My Aunt said,

> *"This will force you into moment- to- moment living. It's a sweet spot in life. Fight to hold onto it."*

I had no idea how hard it would be to stay in that way of living. To live presently, you have to be able to let go of everything outside the moment. My brain is so used to worrying and multi-tasking it was a huge struggle, still is some days…every day since we are totally honest.

Fifteen

Make Your Mess Your Message

I wrote this a few months after my dad died. After what I imagined, my window for grieving had passed. In the aftermath.

Journal Undated Entry 2015

"*MAD, sad, empty, uncontrolled, confused, frustrated, lost, impatient, constantly annoyed. Incomplete.*

- *Romans 7:15, "For the good that I would do, I do not, but the evil which I would not, that I do."*
- *Proverbs 23:7 "So as a man thinketh, so he is in his heart."*
- *James 1:2 "Consider it pure joy, my brothers and sisters, whenever you face trials of many kinds because you know that the testing of your faith produces perseverance. Let perseverance finish its' work so that you may be mature and complete, not lacking in anything."*

I feel so confused with frustration. I don't care why God allowed this to happen. I get all that. The purpose is to get to heaven. The gift is the time to get there. I am thankful for everything, including this pain I feel.

I don't know where it comes from, but I am angry and annoyed too. I just want to be left alone with my thoughts. Alone with my thoughts, I wrestle with them. It's as if I'm daring myself to say what I'm actually thinking. Can I say that?

I don't want to be depressed. I remember looking at momma when Pawpaw died, wondering if she would ever be the same. Seeing pain in her eyes I had never seen before, a sadness where a twinkle once lived. Was it temporary?

I wish I could go away to grieve. There is just so much pressure here. I'm afraid of doing it wrong. Grieving in public is too hard. I don't want to cry in front of the kids. Don't want to talk about it to anyone because I don't want to hear. This is normal. NO, IT ISNT. This is not a normal feeling for me. I don't want to hear you finally broke down, you poor thing, your weak. It feels like everyone's watching to see how I deal. There are no safe places. I feel like I don't have time to grieve, the kids always need something, and I can barely get a thought out. I just want to say leave me alone.

I don't want to ask for help because I want to have it all together. I don't want to be vulnerable. I feel lost. Dad would know just what to say. Having it all together sounds so stupid- so selfish. I would accept help, but I don't know how to ask for it. I don't want help to come with strings. I don't want to owe anyone for being there for me. I don't want them to help me, so they feel better. I don't want to hear about the times they felt like this. These are my moments. Don't hijack them. I feel so protective of my grief. Maybe I'm afraid of hearing these things because I've said to them. I'm sorry.

Everyone thinks I'm fine, strong, handling this so well. How do I be honest and say I'm not. If I ask for help, I'll just be like everyone else. I want to be different, to somehow, in this journey, give hope to others.

Can you grieve gracefully? I don't want to be a beautiful mess. I want to be beautifully in control. I want to cry, but I don't like the pain. None of it changes the fact dad is gone, so why do it. My spirit and my flesh are in a war against each other- knowing it's all about eternity, but wanting him here with me. It's such a strange feeling, I know all the right things, but it doesn't change the way I feel. I'm sad he is not here to laugh with, to Hug, to sing. To talk to. Even fight with. What are these feelings? He was the one I went to when I needed shelter for my heart. Everyone else is grieving too. I feel like I am taking away from their grief when I talk about mine. I just started crying. Caiden and Landon looked over at me and started asking why. I said I'm sad because I miss big daddy. Caiden said you'll see him later and offer me popcorn. I love these boys. They hold space for a moment and then so simply explain it."

* * *

"Make your mess your message." What does it really mean?

Maybe we should start with what it doesn't mean. It is not airing everything out and marching around like a bull in a china shop. Announcing, "here comes the hot mess! Deal or get out of my way." No, I believe the truest way to make your mess your message is to get complete with your mess. Imagine all the energy you are currently using to keep Pandora's box shut. To keep the stuff, you don't know what to do with stuffed inside. Are you there, can you imagine?

Now imagine what you would do, create, dream... who would you be in the world if you used the energy in you to create the life you wish existed instead of using it to keep the bad stuff down. Getting complete allows you to move freely forward, making everything you create, every idea, every thought a direct result of healing. It's producing great things because of what flows out of you, NOT you chasing the next thing to help you feel better about what you are keeping stuffed inside. Here's an example. Writing a book about what you've been through won't heal you. Chasing a piece of legislation to

78

get closure won't complete you.

Banishing people from your life won't make it easier to move forward. These things, while admittedly feel good for a little while, aren't sustainable. They ultimately leave you feeling exhausted, drained, and feeling like you failed once again. You can't outperform YOU. In our incompleteness, we create versions of ourselves to POWER UP. The person you created to deal with your life isn't YOU. It's only a version of you.

Living your life as less than ALL of you is less than what you deserve.

Again, I'm not saying you need to hang your dirty laundry in the town square. I'm saying you've got to find a way to get complete with it. It's a private thing. It does no harm to the ones you love. It restores and rebuilds. It heals. I have given you several places to begin. Your journals, forgiveness, discovering *real* love. What I want you to hear over everything else is it's a process, not an event. There are also lots of methods out there which cater to different personality types. It's less about what method you use and more about what you'll need for the journey.

You'll undoubtedly need to discover your Brave Heart.

Once you are complete with the loss in your life, you will have all you need to start rebuilding. Learning to deal with loss is the bravest thing you can do for the ones you love.

* * *

In previous chapters, I have shared vision statement tools to help keep you focused on the daily choices. It wasn't until someone, or maybe I asked myself once, what do you really stand for? At first, I didn't have an answer. As I grew in my discovery of what was important for the rebuild of my life, I arrived at this.

I stand for being free to show up. I'm a maker of time and an advocate for being with the people who matter. When it matters. I keep believing the world is changed by those who are free to show up! I mean really free. To be completely free, you must be able to show up in 3 areas.

- You must be free to show up in person!! How are you going to show up for people if you have no time freedom?
- Physically. If you are unhealthy- not talking about what you CAN'T control. I'm talking about what you can! The overeating, lack of exercise...
- Emotionally. This is probably one of the most important and difficult. It's the one we make this excuse for. "It's just my personality."

You can arguably connect and leverage the other two with people who have more of the resource you lack, time, money etc. until you have what you need. HOWEVER, the third one. This one is all you. It's the gateway to the others. You must be emotionally free to show up. I'm not talking about allowing everyone to pull up a couch and forcing yourself to listen to everyone. I am talking about being present with whomever you're with, as you both *are* in the moment, without feeling like you have to change each other. FREE from the past, living in the moment.

Making your mess, your message is only possible when you are complete. The first time I had the opportunity to share in a writing workshop with some kids. As children often do, they went right to the jugular.

"What's your book about, Ms. Broadway?" – how do you explain grief to children? Do you share what happened without giving all the details which may not be kid-appropriate? Here's what I learned. We are all little children inside. We must be gentle not to invite more trauma into our lives in the process of rebuilding our lives.

"Well, one day something happened in my life and it made me very sad. Up to that point, I thought life was really fun. I thought I was doing everything right. Then it happened. Something that changed my life forever. I stopped thinking life was fun. I didn't even feel like talking to my friends. So I decided to look down at the ground- a lot. One day I decided to look up again, to see if anything had changed. When I did, I saw lots of sad faces. Their faces looked like my face. I noticed they all seemed to be asking the same question I was. "How do I get to the other side of sad. How do I feel happy again?" So, I decided to take notes about all the things I noticed in the world. I took notes when I felt happy and when I felt sad. I made up games for myself to see if it helped. I recorded what helped and what didn't. In no time at all, things were beginning to change. It worked. So, I took all of my notes and stories that helped, and I put them in a book for other people to read. I help others find their big Brave Hearts and find the other side of sad- I help them find their happy again."

I wasn't entirely sure this would land. Would they get it? Would you? Making your mess, your message is when you can stand in the life you have created, in the healing, not in the identity of what you have been through. And then cheer for others.

Hands shot up, like fireworks on the 4th of July. As if they too were declaring their own independence. I called on one, then another. The same stories, not details, stories. Stories of loss and how they, too, had felt sad. Some were stacks of loss. One on top of the other. In that moment, all I could hear was "Me too."

I had completed the journey of making my mess, my message.

IV

Part Four

The Time to Get it Right
Saying goodbye to the pain is to embrace the freedom.
You are not the sum of what you've been through.
You are NOT defined by the loss you have experienced.
Don't let time slip by spending it wishing things were better,
different, or you had more time.
You can become a maker of time.
Not actually make more time but seeing time as your most
precious resource.
A unique skill, where you stop to notice the world.

Sixteen

What Now?

So what now? Are you feeling a bit like you wished you had a time machine? That you wasted some time? Be encouraged, because you have a heartbeat means you still have time. I hope by now, you have acknowledged that loss walks next to us all the time. The reactions you feel are grief. The limiting beliefs about all of it are what hold you back. I hope you are beginning to challenge those beliefs and step into your transformation.

Saying goodbye to the pain is to embrace the freedom you are not the sum of what you've been through. You are NOT defined by the loss you have experienced.

I hope you have begun to discover who you really are without your layers of protection and whom you belong to. I want you to feel the gift of time. Be intentional and brave to embrace it. Don't let time slip by spending it wishing things were better, different, or you had more time. You can become a maker of time. Not actually make more time but seeing time as your most precious resource. A unique skill, to notice the world. You choose in those moments of conflict, which action which will most in align with the life you want to create.

*I*t was after my 3rd son's birth, yes, three boys, and no, we are not trying for a girl. I started hearing whispers in my soul. "Tell the story."

I am a talker and have been all my life. Every report card I have ever had said to "talks too much in class." It's always noisy in my head, and when I get an idea, I roll with it, journal, talk about it. Rarely, I don't have something to say about something. During my 3rd pregnancy, I had an event I had an event which resulted in a medical condition taking my voice from me for the better part of five months.

A cyst on my vocal folds. It was like a prison. I could speak no louder than a whisper. It took so much energy to speak, so each word had to be chosen with precision. My dad used to say. "**Say what you mean, *mean* what you say.**" This clarity washed over me as I grew in my understanding of what it meant. Choosing our words and getting to the point.

In those months, I also grew a healthy case of voice envy, mine was because I physically couldn't speak, but for you, it may be the different kind. Ever had voice envy? Where someone seemed to be able to say something you couldn't? Feeling disempowered to speak our truth can be a similar kind of prison. The worst part is it's self-inflicted. Well, not consciously anyway, not on purpose. I get it. I did/ do it to myself at times. I get trapped in what might go wrong instead of what might go right. It takes a brave heart to seek the truth, then *say what you mean and mean what you say.* It's a life of consistency and trustworthiness. It's bold.

What if you mess up or change your mind,? You realize you spent all that time saying what you think only to change your mind later. This fear of being an imposter to your life, to be seen as if you *don't* mean what you say. This was a real fear for me when the idea of writing this book began to take shape. What if I get it wrong?

I believe we have a great responsibility to be aware enough to stop in the midst of a trial, and instead of seeing the trial, we see how we can grow through what we are going through. This time was no different, and yet it changed everything. It was a strange awakening to realize how much I relied on my voice, yet how I had taken it for granted, hushed it when it was meant to speak up.

Careless with it. The bible is full of guidance to the power of our words, the blessings and curses they can bring. In these moments of frustration, problem-solving, Dr. appointments. Me trying to fix it. I surrendered.

I remember saying, "fine!!! I guess it's not my turn. Since I can't speak, I guess I'm supposed to listen. What do you want me to hear?"

I spent those months listening and writing responses. I heard him say, "tell the story, write the book." This was so heavy for my heart, I was embarrassed to make such a bold move. Here are a few of my top fears in those moments.

1. Owning, I felt called to write it (what would people think?)
2. It's too big for my people. If I say it out loud, they will have opinions.
3. I was scared, afraid I wouldn't do it and my whole life would end up being a should've, could've, would've.

The last one was a big one. Living with a "maybe next time" mindset only to wake up one day and realize I am out of "next times." Hiding from your dreams is the easy part. There will always be the low hang fruit of excuses ready to fill in the gaps and moments you could have been using to fulfill those dreams. Creating a life you love and moving from wishing to creating take intention. It also takes support. Building a care team, people who care about you and will care for your vision, is a key step in following through. To build a care team, YOU have to take the first step. It will be scary, but you have to say what you've quietly been wishing out loud. Not in a someday I'd like to (fill in the blank) kinda way, but a "today is the day, I'm going to do it" kind of way. Then write it down and pick a date for completion. I do more work on this process in my Moving from Wishing to Creating workshop, but those are the basics. We need a care team who will hold our vision for us. Whisper our truths back to us when we lose our way. Yes, even when you get laser-focused and are full of determination, you will need a care team.

"Sometimes we need to borrow the belief of others until we fully believe in ourselves."

Seventeen

Building your Care Team

⚘⚘⚘

Our Sunday morning bible class was on doing what God calls us to. Mostly centered around being Christ-like. For me, it was the tug I needed. I was super vague when I spoke up. I said something like, it's hard when you feel like God is calling you to something, but you just keep running from it. After class was over, a few friends came over. What are you running from? What's God asking of you? "I think he's asking me to write a book."

I didn't even want to look at their faces. I was afraid I'd be able to read their judgment. Finally, I looked up. She said, "You have to write this book, so I can read it."

She was followed by another who said, "I know He's asking you to write it" We all shed a few tears that morning. Through my crying, I objected again, "But sometimes I say swear words and get life really wrong." I just don't want to be a hypocrite and give more people a reason not to love Him.

"That's what makes you different. You know you're flawed, and you know He loves you."

These ladies have fuelled me, followed up, held me accountable. They were gentle and gracious when I made mistakes. I'm so grateful God chose them to be part of this story of Raising Brave Hearts.

When I told my husband Josh, I'm going to write the book, in his true form, he said. "Love it. Do it. Can't wait." My husband is very to the point. He models for me how you don't have to say everything you're thinking. I'd like to say I model for him how to say what you're thinking, but I can't speak for him. He has been a champion for me in the most consistent of ways. Always there to affirm and challenge me, to be sure I am convicted in what I want. Sometimes you need to be challenged by your care team to have to defend your cause. Speak up and gain clarity in why you want more for you and those around you.

* * *

Borrowing the belief of others

The more I objected to writing this, the louder the voice grew. The more obstacles I found, the more I heard do it anyway. And then there was this moment. Leave it to social media to tip the scales. The hubs and I were sitting on the couch together and scrolling social. A quiz pops up.

"How well do you know your spouse?" -See, God can use social media-lol.

I selected it for some fun and giggling, said, "Ok, you're up. How well do you know me? Are you ready?"

"Ok, he says. Give it to me." A few standard questions, favorite candy, color, and then this one.

"If your spouse was going to be famous for something, what would it be. "

A pause... He says, "The book"

Really? - you think people will read it? A tone of objection in my voice. I adjust my relaxed position, untangling my legs from his lap and leaning closer to hear his insight. My husband is a man of few words. I guess it's what makes what he has to say so powerful.

"Yes, sweetheart. I think they would read what you have to say."

While I still object to the idea I will be "famous," what I heard was, I believe in you, and it was the hug my heart needed.

You might be thinking, "Wait isn't this book about raising Brave Hearts? Why is she afraid?"

I'm afraid because I'm human. Being brave isn't the absence of doubt, fear, rejection. It's doing it anyway. It's also called a *journey to...*, implying I'm still on the path. I'm still learning when to aspire and when to inspire. I am really learning *that* aspiring IS inspiring.

The thing about being brave is it lets you show up and embrace your voice. When you arrive at this vulnerable place, you find a new space full of hope. Part of what I want deeply is to be sure YOU have a place to rise to. Not everyone who shares their dreams has support.

> *"When you embrace your Brave Heart, I want you to have a community*
> *waiting to embrace you. Raising Brave Hearts in each other is just as*
> *important as raising our own.*
> *It starts with you {me} and grows into us."*

Eighteen

Get Clarity

R emember, "Say what you mean, mean what you say," in noticing how precious the spoken word is, I also learned the power of the written. The written is forever. Holding space for your ideas, hopes, and dreams; there to remind you when you lose your way. Holding you accountable to embracing life. I learned how much of what I had been speaking was like filler in a bouquet of flowers. Looks pretty and definitely has a place, but it's not the roses.

"Getting a bouquet is beautiful and welcomed.
Getting a single rose makes the point. It says I chose THIS one for you.
In the forced silence and the listening,
I saw the magnitude of being purposeful with how we speak to one
another.
"Say what you mean, MEAN what you say."

We most definitely leave people incomplete with our intentions. We say one thing without thinking and then follow up with, "Oh, I didn't mean that." Please don't waste time saying what you don't mean. The word intention is best used as an action, not an excuse. Set intentions for who you will be even *when* the world gets crazy, not excusing the way you were understood.

Maybe you've heard the phrase "The power of the pause," The power of the pause is a moment of intention. It's when YOU choose what comes next. It's hardest to do when you're running your mouth in the heat of the moment. That is also when it's the most powerful. The ability to stop, notice, and choose opens a new world for you. It's a pivotal moment in transitioning from being someone who overcomes struggles to someone who rises and solves problems with the end in mind.

Undated journal entry

...it started as a whisper, and now it's coming through a bullhorn. This reminder- I didn't follow through. I don't know why I said no- I suppose it was mostly because I wasn't intentional- which can be the same as saying NO. It's easier to make excuses than to own saying NO.

Wanting more for your life is a luxury many people don't feel like they can afford because they don't have a plan to get there. It feels frivolous to want for something you have no idea how to get. In my years in building networks and marketing them, the same thing consistently revealed itself. When I asked what goals you have, they were short-sighted for the most part. Breakthroughs only came when they were brave enough to speak about the life they WISH they had, then trust the process enough to create a plan. When I said yes to writing this, it was hard not to get sucked into more how-to manuals, instructional ways to change instead of following my heart. The best opportunities in life will always be where you see a good idea, AND you see yourself participating. If you can't dream it, you won't do it. Dreams are never logical they are all heart.

Surrounding yourself with people who will hold an anchor for you to dream is essential. Who will dream with you? Notice and wonder how it will come to fruition. When we had no money, we had more money than ever. We sat and dreamt and lived our lives in the vision of what we created.

Reality was just the path we were taking to get to where our dreams were. Organization was the road map, the plan to get there. Plan the work and then WORK the plan.

Excuses are a luxury you can't afford when building your dreams. They are a block to progress. You'll do better to own your "I don't want to" than to dance around with which excuse sounds the most convincing, the most logical.

My lack of progress writing this book, was yes, in part, I wasn't ready and had more things to learn. It was also a fear of rejection. Being too bold. Fear of what comes next. Fear of more loss. God, and I went round and round over this. Yes, I argue with God. I talk out loud in protest, and He finds a way to whisper truth right back to my heart. Usually through a friend or piece of writing. Sometimes through my own journals. It is a weird feeling, by the way. When you're inspired by yourself. When you realize, Wowza! You're not that bad. (insert sarcasm) when you see yourself the way, others see you. When you honor your own potential and start talking to yourself like a friend instead of your own worst enemy, it's special and sacred. The first member of your care team needs to be YOU. Embrace that.

Excuses are for people who are stuck in the opinion of what others think they should be doing with their life. They exist to defend us and are completely useless because they suck you right back into a life of comparison. "Is my excuse good enough to justify my lack of action?" If you know you want something, and you're not ready to take action? **Own that**! I really want to insert a curse word, but I think you get my point.

Taking responsibility for where you are and where you want to go is all you. NO one can do it for you. Taking responsibility will, for sure, feel uncomfortable. It will also be the only motivation you need to take a step forward. Trust me. When you realize the only thing stopping you is YOU. It's a new kind of freedom. No more opinion to battle, no more rat race. JUST you and your dreams waiting to be fulfilled. MY joy is getting to come alongside you and fan the flame. To encourage you and to build a community of Brave Hearts where you are safe and find inspiration for your journey.

* * *

A few notes for you from my journal about building your dreams:

You are what makes you, YOU.

We don't compare apples to oranges.
Why compare people. We are all so uniquely the US.

NO credentials will help you tell your story.
You are the expert on you.

Look for the "and moments."
Don't spend time in "either" - it's too limiting.

"I either choose this or this"
Replace with "I can do this AND This"

You will then see an opportunity to create something you wish you
had.
It's how all great ideas start.

Help others say me too, not so what.
Connect the dots and be open to change

Don't audit your life; LIVE it.

Nineteen

A Million Dreams Outside Your Comfort Zone

*I*f you're going to create a life you love, you've got to be willing to embrace the weird.

The greatest showman swept the country in 2018. It seemed everywhere you looked, kids and adults were singing their hearts out and filling their homes with a million dreams and endless possibilities. The soundtrack played on repeat in our home only to be replaced by the movie when it was released. I remember sitting in the theatre by myself watching it for the first time. Tears were rolling as my heart filled with inspiration. It will be a favorite forever.

Even our school theme that year was THE GREATEST ME, a celebration of becoming the best version of YOU and embracing what makes you, YOU.

When a circus-themed birthday party based on The Greatest Showman meets a non-Halloween excuse to wear costumes. The Broadway's get excited.

Everyone was encouraged to dress up. The day arrived, and I dug out a red carnival appropriate dress from a previous costume, got out my top hat complete with a feather plume, high heel, glitter booties, and topped it off with some dramatic red lipstick. The kids went to the nine's as well. As we crossed the grass to the front door, the awareness other guests were not dressed up washed over me like the ice bucket challenge of 2014.

"Boys! Maybe I shouldn't have dressed so over the top."

"Why, Mom??" They objected as though my hesitation was so absurd. Because I'm feeling nervous, I feel like I stand out and I'm out of my comfort zone.

I was willing to go big when I'm in MY zone, at MY house. I love creating a space where it's ok to come as over the top or weekend sweatpants ready, and you'll be perfect for the occasion. BUT this wasn't my space. It was someone else's. Thoughts running through my head were, what if my bold was too bold for them?? The host had indicated she would be dressed up also, so I was holding out for at least there would be two of us.

Can you imagine my surprise when she answered the door in very normal clothes? Before I knew it, my mouth was open, and I was nervously explaining and justifying the way I was dressed. I'm pretty sure I apologized for dressing up {insert palm hitting forehead emoji}

As we went in, there wasn't really anyone dressed up. At that moment, I felt out of place. Like I should have downplayed it. Dialed it in!. Like my crazy was showing, and I needed to tuck it in. It was a spiral of second-guessing myself. Have you ever noticed, ladies, how high heels make you walk with a statement? You can't walk in heels and not be heard, seen. Heels make you walk on purpose. You make a statement and deliberately. There is no way to walk casually in heels. Especially glittery stiletto booties. Me tiptoeing around, trying not to make noise was awkward. A teachable visual moment!

You, trying not to be seen by the world,
is harder to watch than if you just did it, owned it.

I remembered I Had flip flops in the car, and I got out of the heels.

Blend in when you need to, but don't forget you were born to stand out.

The shoe change made all the difference for me. It made it more comfortable to spend the day committed to the costume. They might be able to see me, but at least I can be quiet about it, lol. I need to share I also didn't allow this to ruin the whole event. It didn't consume me, though I was painfully uncomfortable for a bit.

What a cherished, eye- opening lesson this day was. Here's what I got extra that day.

You've got to want something even if you're the only one doing it.

It can't be because of someone or something else. Yes, it's easier with community in moments where it's an "all play," BUT the *want to* has to be yours. You've got to take ownership of it. It's ok to be the only one.

Shoes definitely make or break the outfit. I was shocked how much my shoes changed my attitude, lol.

It's more fun to love out loud and on purpose
than to blend in,
taking the less exceptional road

UNLESS you're an introvert, and the idea of blending in sets your soul on fire, then BE THAT. Own it, embrace it. For heaven's sake, don't apologize or defend it.

My point is you should be who you are and DO the things you love because it fills you. It feels like the most authentic true version of you. *Wear those shorts, girl.* Living on purpose is the key to being known and loved for you.

It's to be seen and known- which by the way, you can be *seen and known* as an introvert too... It's belonging and being different at the same time.

Living this way lets others appreciate and trust you because they know what they are getting. It builds community and relationships. It's an accelerant to accomplishing great things when you trust yourself to be you, and others trust you are real and you'll show up.

To be yourself in the face of change- in the presence of adversity, when you're the only one. Your Brave Heart says, "It's ok. I will go first."

For me, I'd rather be known for being willing to go first, be known for my courage, and be all used up- the good kind of empty from helping others discover their own path and cheering them to the best version of living.

When I leave this earth, I want to be known for my courage to take the road less traveled, full of new experiences. I want to be known for my Brave Heart. It's worth it because it helps others feel like they can too.

* * *

One of my early DIY exercises in embracing the things I love and making them work together was at Halloween. It was my first year coordinating the church trunk or treat. I was so focused on the event, I was delayed in getting my own outfit together. Do you do that too? I had inspiration pieces laying all out, trying to fit them together. Then it came over me. Why not all the things. The ultimate {AND} moment to embrace creating what I wish existed.

I'll wear it all! It was such a fun moment. If I liked it... I wore it!! For real. I had a stunning pair of feather angel wings, my favorite earrings, shoes (don't forget the shoes), eyelashes... the works. When I arrived, I got questions? "So help me with your costume?" Laughing, I said it's all of me. These are a few of my favorite things. - In hindsight, I would have made a cute sign to put on my back or something.

I loved it as much as others got a kick out of the uniqueness of it. I'm inviting you to go to all your favorite things next year for Halloween or host a dinner party with all your favorite foods, New Year's bash with a favorite's theme. We have even used this theme at birthday parties. I make all their favorites from the year, and we decorate with all the phases of toys, etc. It's nostalgic, fun, and EASY.

Having a celebration for people to be all of themselves, and it's not weird. Is really fun! Try it. If all this sounds totally terrifying, it is ok. Love the life YOU love right now without regret. Don't get surprised by the oops. It's too late. You missed it moments. Embrace the time you have to get it right. It's a gift. We don't get do-overs, so; hug now, love now, and at the end, I think in those final moments of life, when we get to heaven, one of life's big questions just might be,

Why didn't you wear heels to the party?

* * *

Take away application:

The how-to always raises its ugly head. You get fired up, and then HOW shows up and asks you to prove how bad you want "this." Here's a few tips if you find yourself feeling like you need to find a how-to in order to fulfill your why. When you feel forced to pick between two hard choices. For example, I really want to take a weekend away for personal development, BUT I can't because my family needs me. I can speak to this one, especially. I will tread lightly, but I want you to hear this. These are the best AND moments. The ones you get to create what you wish existed. Forced to accept either or and you chose **AND**.

This tip is similar to when we did the vision statement exercise. It's meant to slightly shift your perspective and help you view what might be possible.

- To begin, you have to decide to do it! -write out exactly what you want to do, remember- no limits.
- Answer this question: What would it look like to do **This** and **That**? What you want and a responsibility which you have been using as an excuse.
- Next, Identify the **can't- the reasons you can't have both.**

Again for me, it once was. I want to be home with my kids, but I need the extra income from my job. The Can't was: *You Can't quite your job because you need the insurance, the money, etc.* So, I settled for something less than

99

what I really wanted.

The breakthrough was creating an AND moment. I saw a gap in my life - not being fulfilled in my journey as a mom and wanting to be home with my kids. I decided to fill it with an *"AND opportunity."*

My "and" was how can you stay home AND earn a paycheck. Being willing to dream outside what I thought was possible, using those questions to guide me, I began searching for opportunities that ONLY resulted in me fulfilling my *and* moment. It was tough at first because all I saw were more excuses as to why I couldn't have it. You need a commitment to yourself to get in there and do whatever it looks like to **you**. Remember, no comparison, and while you care about others, you are free from their opinion. Try these out. I bet when you get clear on why you want 'it' all kinds of fun *and* moments will show up.

The final step to embracing this mindset shift, if you haven't already guessed it is people. Once you're clear on the '*and*' you want to create, you'll need to declare it. Invite others to help you create something that once did not exist for you. You'll be surprised at how many people want to be part of something bigger than themselves.

Twenty

Taking Turns

ven when you decide, and you have a clearly defined vision. You can still feel blocked.

I can't get any traction in my ideas.
Why am I stalled? Are you sure it's me, God?

This is something I would say to myself. Almost as if being blocked meant I hadn't chosen the right path. Have you ever felt like that? It's hard to know what is a temporary problem due to timing and what is a game-changing flashing detour sign you are on the wrong path. Here's what I will propose. Consider this; If you haven't figured out your next move, nothing is *wrong;* it's because it's not your turn. It's His. Read the last sentence again.

There is probably something you are meant to learn. I used to get frustrated every time I felt stuck. You can ask my mom about me trying to put clothes on a baby doll when I was 4. Thankfully, it was not a preview of my parenting skills. Being frustrated is expected and is ok; Letting your frustration be your reason for quitting is not ok. When I first started out in my home-based business, I spent a year chasing different success strategies not to grow and learn but to get unstuck. If you were pan out to a wide shot of my life, like the helicopter shots you see in a news report, I used to be the crazy person driving the getaway car swerving all over the highway trying to find the exit. Maybe that's a little extreme, but you get the idea.

It resulted in a lack of momentum, bouncing around from idea to idea only to end up with no progress. Once again, I had traded my heart for a how-to manual and began living inside other people's opinions of what my business should look like. What I needed was someone to stop me and say, it's not your turn. I needed to surrender my pride, open my eyes, shred the how-to manual, and embrace my heart again. In the process of writing this book, there were many times I stopped and waited my turn. Seeking reflection and learning opportunities rather than bouncing from idea to idea. This mindset is best described as *staying in your lane, which* brings me to another type of excuse we often make for not following through.

Someone else is already doing what I want to do. If I can't be original, why bother. Please just drop that way of thinking. We are all so uniquely different. Your unique fingerprint belongs on the project. Make your make. EVEN if you and I were to write the same book about raising brave hearts, you would have totally different stories to share as an example of what that looks like. Honoring the stories of our lives is so important.

Too often, I hear at funerals, "I had no idea the impact they made. I didn't know they thought that; did that." Sharing how you see the world is a gift to the world. Your opinions and what you notice should be shared. We all have contributions to give. Just because it wasn't your idea doesn't mean you don't get to share in the joy of bringing it to life. Finding a cause to be a part of, to champion, is a great first step to finding your own mark you'll make. For me, I joined the cause of inspiring others.

> *Learning to stay in your lane means you acknowledge*
> *some desires laid on your heart aren't meant for you.*
> *They are part of someone else's journey.*
> *They were given to you to care of*
> *until you notice where they belong.*

You do not have to take on every idea you ever have. We are all connected; Sometimes, you are the messenger. You also have to embrace this. Be willing to speak out loud, the desires of your heart. It's all part of the plan. Don't fall into the "figure it out trap." You'll be left wondering or saying, WHY God, why did you put this on my heart just to not give me a plan for it. Sharing it with others might be exactly what your part is. How it works out is how everyone comes together.

* * *

Nothing risked, nothing gained. Now is the time to be brave. I acknowledged the need to stay in my lane, accepting my lane was to create. To create the content, write the stories, bring people together, create the vision, create costumes, create answers for problems. I only need to learn how to do my job. Embrace my gifts, and be willing to put my fingerprint on the projects. He has faithfully merged my lane with the right people every time, this book being no exception. In only the ways He can. In the God moments. My most successful business moments are when I share the vision, do the inviting, and then turn it over to a team member. It's worth mentioning where ever you are starting out, business or personally, there will be a time where you have to do it all because you simply don't have the team yet. I used to do events by myself until I had a team. Then I had to consciously choose to stay in my lane and do what I was good at. Over the years, we have built a team of people who are good at all different things, but together we all had in common was we wanted more. In my relationships, especially instead of doing it all, I use my energy to be me, not them. I focus on embracing who I am so they know who they can count on when I'm needed. If you are wishy-washy about your role, how will anyone know who to ask when they need what only you can bring to the table?

Twenty-One

Learning to Ask Big

⟊⟊⟊

I n Scotland, they have a long tradition of gala days. Not as popular in larger cities, as I imagine it's not practical. In Livingston village, they were still booming. Every year a royal party was chosen from the community by way of nominations. The remainder of the community would gather in celebration on the day, dressing in costumes. A bit like our Halloween, but not scary. This was also a time before buying costumes was much of an option. The costume judging was cash prizes. Our family is almost always placed. My mom was her own Pinterest board.

Pinning ideas from the people she met and collaborating with people she knew. This is not a dig at Pinterest. I love and am inspired by it. Just a shout out to those of us who grew up in a world before it. If you are chosen, you would join the other members of the royal party in decorating our homes for the parade. On the day of the event, there would be a float tour, and everyone would pile in the big floats and drive around the village touring the homes. There is a judging process for the homes as well. It's quite a to-do. The rest of the day is spent in the village competing in the gala games: high jumps, sack races, highland dancing, craft show. There are picnic blankets as far as you can see. It is a spirit of community.

Nomination day had come and gone. I had no expectations of being chosen.

Although, what a dream it would be. You see, I didn't think I was *that* little girl. I didn't consider myself pretty. My eczema covered my body. Even my face. Although I have seen much worse as I've grown up. For me, it was enough to self-label as not pretty enough for something such as a gala girl.

"Jessica, you have mail." She called. 10-year olds don't get mail unless it's important and on purpose. I couldn't believe it. Some well-meaning soul had nominated me for a lady in waiting. Was it a mistake? I didn't even care who had nominated me. It could have been my own mother, all that mattered was I was chosen. The following days were full of excitement. Dress fitting, shoe shopping, and Oh My! What will our theme be for our home and garden presentation? I was so into barbies at the time. Our neighbor had an amazing custom-built dollhouse. It was glorious. Every chance I got, I wanted to be at her house playing with it.

Several Christmases later, I became the owner of that dollhouse, but at the time, it filled my world with adventures in Barbie Land. Barbie Land! Yes! "Mum, Can we do Barbie Land?" "Barbie Land?" she objected. "Sweetheart, we don't have enough Barbie stuff for a whole land of Barbies." "We can try," I remember pleading. Whenever my kids say the phrase "we can try" I flashback to the moment, I intensely believed it was possible. She borrowed, bought, and scrounged every barbie she could come up with, and yet when we filled the seemingly tiny front garden, it seemed like Yellowstone for the Barbies.

When my mom tells this story, she talks about how nervous she was to take the leap. To dream, fearing the disappointment of a "No." She had an idea to write a letter to Mattel asking for demo barbies. Samples or whatever they could spare. She explained our cause and what we hoped to accomplish. Letter sent our hearts nervously waiting for a reply, the days counting down. It's hard to wait on an answer. The day came. A GIANT box, really it was as tall as my little sister arrived on the front steps.

We had a 2-step front door, which was home to freshly delivered milk every morning. The box consumed the space, which made it appear even larger. WHAT could it be? I have to say. I'm the luckiest kid to experience such magic. They said YES in a big way. All brand-new barbies, BBQ sets, pools, stables, horses, and my favorite; A red convertible Ferrari. They had most definitely NOT answered with junk. No, they answered with more than we could possibly have imagined. Life has afforded me many moment's some less than expected, some more than I could have imagined. This was one of the Brave Heart moments, where we asked big and received big.

We didn't win first place, but that morning I was so proud of all the day meant. I stood in front of the full-length mirror in my parent's room, waiting for the town car to arrive. I remember holding out the sides of my dress in a swaying motion to ensure it was perfect. My mom came in. "Your car is here." What 10-year-old gets that greeting? Seriously so LUCKY.

"Mum, can I tell you something? I feel like the ugly duckling that gets to be a swan for the day." I don't remember her crying, but if it had been me hearing those words from my child, I would have lost it. She simply hugged me and said, you're always a swan, but today people get to see you how I see you. She was good at that, not overshadowing the moment. It wasn't about her, and she let me have the moment. In my boldness and life out loud style, I pray to find ways to let my kids have their moments. Moments where they hear their *own* voice first and hear mine as affirmation.

That was a big year for all of us. Incidentally the last year, we would get to be part of the gala day festivities. It was a day I learned to ask big. It's ok to be afraid of the answer, it's not ok to not ask. Don't be silent, practical, or reserved in your asks.

Be bold, challenge your expectations, and reach just beyond what you think is possible.

Thank you, Mom.

Twenty-Two

A Brave Heart Tells the Truth

⁓ ∽

*"A **Brave Heart** isn't afraid to remember*
so they can live forward."

Growing up, the adults in my life would comfort me with the phrase Sticks and stones. I've shared how unkind kids can be. I had many peer reviews regarding the way I looked.

"Sticks and stones may break my bones, but words will never hurt me."

I'm positive I'm not the first to share how ridiculous this statement is. I hate it. It represents the opposite of authentic living. "Never hurt me?" Hear this, You cannot stop hurt. Hurtful things people do and say will never not hurt. YOU do choose whether the pain stops you. Whether it impacts your choices or whether you say. "That hurt. I'm not letting it stop me." Ignoring the pain is to cut out a part of your soul. To wall up and power through. It sounds easier, but in the long run, it's soul-crushing. We were designed to feel it all. The lie we buy into is we have to allow every feeling we have to choose what comes next. Just take a moment. What feelings do you allow to choose for you? Is it getting out of bed? Loving the unlovable? I live and breathe the power of choice. I know full well you can't live a life governed by the opinion of others.

If you're living your life according to everyone else's opinion, is it really YOUR life?

So, how come, 20+ years post sticks and stones, I find myself out in the middle of summer in yoga pants? I greet my friend with a wave and head across the street to the playground. This was a rowdy day for my crew, and little Macklan was still in the 'I'm too big to carry, but not big enough to walk across the street phase,' so I hoisted him on to my hip with all the other mom accessories and motioned for the kids to grab on to something as we crossed the road.

Eventually, we made it to our friends and the kids scattered to embrace the day's adventure. My friend and I grabbed a spot in the shade, and almost as soon as she said, "Hello," she said, "Why are you wearing pants? It's 100 degrees outside. I shrugged and said something like."

"Oh, I don't wear shorts." To which she replied,

"Girl, you gotta get over that. It's too hot."

It bugged me all day how easily she said, "Get over it." I couldn't remember why I stopped wearing shorts. What did I need to get over? I didn't have any reason other than not liking how they looked. Then it hit me. I remembered! I laughed and then cried, thinking how silly it was.

One day in gym class, A friend came to me with a secret message from a boy I had a crush on. Eager to hear what he said about me, we huddled in a corner. "I Don't know if I should tell you," she said. Clapping my hands excitedly, I assured her anything was better than nothing. "Tell ME!"

"Weeellll... she stretched it out f-o-r- e-v-e-r! "He said you're nice, but your legs look like mash potatoes. They are kinda. WHITE and LUMPY." It was a movie moment. Time froze for me as everything blurred into the background.

She kept talking, but I couldn't hear her. The nervous panic of how I will keep from running out of gym class, how will I stop my face from showing I know what he said. How do I hide?

My impressionable heart decided then to protect me. I would no longer wear shorts.

I wouldn't be where I am today if I didn't fully realize this moment was an innocent one. The kid didn't know he would impact my decisions for the next 20 years. *I* certainly didn't know it would. Had someone stopped that moment and said to me, "be careful what you think next, it will impact the next 20 years." I would have laughed and said, *"NO WAY, Only someone with half a brain would change because of what someone said to them."*

TRUTH is we only have half a brain. We are constantly being tossed back and forth by opinion as we strive to find our truth and place in the world.

"Tell the truth about yourself all the time."

It's not in the times we get it right. It's the **time** we have to get it right. What you do with time is impacted by the tools you have to get you there.

Brave hearts aren't afraid to go back and re-evaluate where they lost the truth and began living inside the lie. Living inside the lie means you can't see it. You don't even know it's there, choosing FOR you every day. What was once meant as a safety net? Temporary protection to help you take the next step has now become who you are. You can't stop smart people from saying dumb things. However, you can decide when you stop listening.

I was 35 when I discovered I was listening to that lie and 35 years and a minute older when I decided to stop living in it.

I went right in my closet, grabbed a pair of jeans, cut them off, and wore shorts to the store that afternoon.

Did I immediately love my legs again? NOPE!

Did I want to set myself free? YES!

It was hard not to beat myself up or feel silly for having avoided shorts for so long. Chances are you have something you feel silly about too; Something if you told others, they would say..: "That's ridiculous, GIRL, you need to get over that." Forgive yourself, then confess. Confession is good for the soul and is permission to let go of the lie, say goodbye to the pain, and start living in truth. Living forward.

Sharing what you learned does 3 things:

1. Holds you accountable to living your truth.
2. Cleanses the soul and is a path to healing
3. {HOPEFULLY} encourages someone else to find their truth too.

While you are not perfect, you are still WORTHY. Nothing can change that. Brave hearts tell the truth, seek the truth, and allow the truth to set them free.

They are also a million degrees cooler in the summer because Brave Hearts wear the shorts. They wear the lipstick they love, that someone said was too bold. They wear fancy dress *even* if it means they or overdressed for the party.

Maybe it's not the dress, or the lipstick or even the shorts for you. But it's something. What are you not doing that you'd love to do because secretly, you're stuck in the weight of what others will think? I spent too much time SAYING I don't care what people think, which was a lie. Sticks and stones thinking... It led me down a road which felt fake and guarded. Like I was floating in a sea being tossed around, having to FIGHT to hold on to what I wanted in my life. Sometimes going under for a while, unseen. You can't POWER through life. You can't overcome it. You can't pretend it doesn't leave a mark on you.

I learned I am and forever will be someone who accepts I care deeply for what others think. I now also know I can care what they think without letting WHAT they think impact the way I live.

Brave Hearts know you get one life, and when it's over… You can say I did it, not I wish I did. Sometimes you don't even remember why we stopped being or doing something we loved. Take it back, be you, and enjoy life.

Cheers to you.

Use this space to write some of your truths. Then find a friend to share them with. Say "here are some truths about me and what I what for my life, thank you for listening"

Twenty-Three

Drop of faith

"A brave heart knows when to let go"

Have you ever been so close to something and panicked because you couldn't see the next move? Suspended in-between what you know and what you don't know?

That was my Caiden. Moments earlier, he had pulled a small step stool over to the coffee table in a fashion only an 18-month chubby legged toddler can. Once he felt it was adequately placed, he stood back, sizing up the job. I could see the wheels turning in his mind as he figured out how to turn a coffee table into a stage. Then all at once, he hoisted himself up, swinging a leg up to assist the pull up onto the surface of the table. Triumphantly he raised both hands and was practically glowing with pride. "I DO IT," he boomed.

At that time in our life, we owned a condo which was the result of a great "before kids" idea. Two kids in, we had no back yard and two very active boys. Their back yard was quite literally our living room. They have always climbed on tables, jumped off couches, and, yes, even road bikes in the hallway. I often referred to this time as feeling like I lived in a circus, complete with frequent costume changes and performances.

This day was no different, other than instead of being a cheerleader watching them play, I was pouting. I don't even remember what I was so funked-out about. I just remember laying on the couch praying somewhere between; please don't break your arm and please let this activity occupy you for more than 5 minutes. As you may know, toddlers are busy humans...this was likely his umpteenth activity for the morning. I also recall watching him with a degree of longing.

He had zero problems to conquer outside of where his focus was. He was present to the moment at hand. He is not worried about lunch, bills, or any of that nonsense. Just focused intently on living his biggest, best life and bravely going where no toddler had gone before. The top of the coffee table.

The free-spirited glow he had was calling to me that day. I wanted to answer-really I did, but I just couldn't. After what seemed to be 3 hours in the mind of a toddler, 5 seconds to his momma, he was done. He plopped his diapered bum down in the middle of the table and scooted to the edge, flipped over on his tummy, and scooted back some more. He scooted until his arms were outstretched as far as they could go without releasing the sides of the table. Legs dangling in the air, toes wiggling fiercely, trying to find the top of the stool.

He repeated this up, down, scoot drill for several minutes. Each time growing in frustration. By this time, my funky mood was no longer driving me. I was very much engaged in watching him solve this problem. He finally stands up on the table, arms stretched out, pleading with me to come to get him down. AGAIN, you must know this is a second child, lesson learned scenario. If I get up and help him, it will become a new game of; what can I climb up on and have Mom get me down. NO, I was sure I did not need any new games in our house. I go through the normal mom checklist. Is he in physical danger? Do I have time to wait patiently? Is he emotionally safe? - you may get the first 2. The second you may need to read again. Is he emotionally safe? This is a checklist item for me. There are times when a child is FAR too vulnerable to teach them a lesson. Not every moment is teachable. If we don't pause to inventory this, we risk bruising a spirit, breaking trust, and adding anxiety.

* * *

This is true for us when they are grown up too. Sometimes we are far too vulnerable to learn a lesson. We replace the screening question "Am I emotionally safe for learning?" with a criticism of how we screwed up. Then it becomes. "See, I told you so" or "What did you think was going to happen," or how about, "When will you ever learn?" UGH, it breaks my heart to even type this. We are so hard on our kids, ourselves, and each other.

So, I'm sure you are on pins and needles about my suspended little Caiden, right? He was trying to get off the table and was mere inches from the footstool, but he didn't know it. I kept insisting he just let go. You're almost there, bud. He just couldn't let go. He is too young to know what trust in action looks like, so saying, trust me. Means nothing. He doesn't even know he trusts me. Raising my voice only raises the bar of anxiousness. So, there he is, just hanging on for dear life, thinking he is doomed to plummet hundreds of feet, and the worst part...he manages to stammer out in his little 2-year-old voice. Mommy, don't let me fall.

Ugh. Heart-wrenching. I would never LET you fall. You are so close. All you need is the drop of faith. "Let go. You're almost there. You can do it. Don't give up."

It took all my strength not to do it for him. I get up and move toward him. I am now close to his face. "Let go, buddy. You can do this. The stool is right there."

In a split second, he released his white-knuckled grip. The second he let go was the second his toes touched the stool. This infinite look of joy and relief filled his face. "I did it, I did!" He chants.

"Yes, you did, my brave boy. Yes, YOU did."

It doesn't matter to him I KNEW he could do it. That wasn't what got him to let go. What got him to let go was his Brave Heart. Emphasis on <u>HE let go</u>. I can only take credit for being there for him. It still required him to take action.

* * *

Taking action requires 'The faith drop.' You've heard the leap of faith? It's usually pictured as someone jumping over a huge gap. The understanding is they are willing to jump, even if they are not certain, they can make it. The thing about the leap of faith is you usually know where you're leaping to. You may doubt if you can make it. However, you usually know what you're leaping towards.

What if you have no idea what you're shooting for? You haven't found out what you want to do yet. You're still holding on to old tools trying to use them to build a new life. You're not even sure you know far you have to go. What if you can't see the other side even to begin to take the leap of faith? This is the faith drop when you have no idea what is next or how far you'll have to go. This is the moment you feel the stirring in your heart to go big, to quit your job and start your own business. To be PTA president even though you are still trying to figure out what PTA actually does. Saying Yes to a new relationship, even though you are afraid of being hurt. Forgiving the unforgivable. These are the moments you don't know what's next, but you know action is necessary.

These are the moments you answer with YES, Lord. That's it. Just a Yes, and then you let go. You can't figure them out and then say yes. You can't say yes and then dig your heels in. You most definitely can't pray for change and then blame God for not answering it. You have to be willing to say YES, then take the drop of faith, knowing He wouldn't ask you to do it if all you were going to do was fail. He does not write desires, hopes, and dreams on our hearts just to watch us fail. Although we are great at blaming Him for "failure," it is actually not a failure at all. We never took action, never even tried. We made excuses and thought a lot about it but never created any results. He doesn't need to teach us lessons, so we know He's right. He just has this perfect love for us. He wants us to trust him enough to drop.

When we are brave enough to say YES, Lord, and let go, we can experience the freedom which comes in witnessing how faithful He is and how brave we really are.

Caiden Broadway, age 2

Twenty-Four

Maker of Time

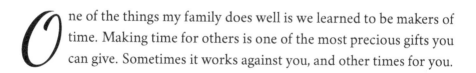

"A Brave Heart creates time"

Have you ever had a moment you wish was different? Specifically, someONE was different. Maybe the person you did with our forgiveness exercise? Have you thought to yourself, I wish they would just defy reasoning and there would be this grand gesture, a bold declaration which would define how much they care for me? Your own real-life magic of the movie's moment?

O ne of the things my family does well is we learned to be makers of time. Making time for others is one of the most precious gifts you can give. Sometimes it works against you, and other times for you.

"Are you telling me you're not coming, but you really plan on showing up? Because my hopes are getting high, I need to know what world to walk in fantasy or reality."

I've said this a time or two. I'm a dreamer. My go-to is always to dream big. That phrase in one form or another is our kill switch. If that question gets asked, you have to answer it.

We hold each other's dream gently. We are a show-up *family, even when things are bad.*

We have a history of grand gestures and fun memories, so it's natural for us to expect greatness all the time. We have also practiced being honest and honoring each other's expectations. We've learned to share a vision of what we want, even if the answer is no. If the answer is no, this time, it lands peacefully with us because of what happens next. We gift each other the space to voice what we wish it could be like. Sometimes there are tears, most always laughter. We acknowledge it's not always possible to defy reality and create magic. It's ok.

It's ok to say no. It's not ok to pretend "no" is not disappointing.

I was 29 nearing my 30th birthday. I was feeling particularly empty. It was about a week before my birthday, and all I really wanted was togetherness. My Caiden was six months old, and I was feeling more and more stretched. I just longed for one of those mom hugs and some sister time. A quiet day reflecting. As the week went on, I knew this was less and less likely to be the case. My mom was working full-time and had an odd and crazy shift. One of those schedules which made it nearly impossible for her to make it to me and get back. Dad was busy with a project, and both of my sisters had tiny babies of their own.

* * *

Sometimes life is just this way. We're all stretched so thin it's all we can do to keep together without splitting.

Resigning to this, my mom went with a fun new tradition. For those who are far away. She would bake their favorite cake and then call them singing happy birthday. The night before my birthday, I called to say how much I was regretful of the circumstances, how I hoped we could make a better plan for the future to be more purposeful with birthdays. I don't know if turning 30 had me freaked or just a sense of time is passing fast. Here I was on the eve of my 30th birthday, and my sweet husband was doing his best to add comfort to my tender heart. I was having a party alright, a pity party and everyone was invited… Disappointment is a hard thing to balance.

Someone told me once, disappointment was a luxury I couldn't afford. He wasn't wrong. It's one thing to feel sad. Disappointment can lead to a lack of action. It can freeze you. It traps you ruminating on what you wish was better, or different, or you wish you had more of; it's incomplete.

That night all I could think of was how I wish I had more time; I wish I had a private plane. I wished things were different. I was not present with my sadness. I was everywhere else. To add to my disappointment, I was still working outside the home at the time and had an awful schedule with breast-feeding and pumping. For the 4th time that morning, the baby woke me around 6 AM on a non-workday. Happy Birthday to me, I whispered. Y'ALL, if you're a Momma, I hope you can relate. It's a hard journey. Sleepless nights, juggling careers, making sure everyone else is cared for. I was in a tough season. My soul felt weary. I didn't know how to fill my cup- yet.

I went into the living room, sitting down, rocking the little one, getting ready to feed him. My chair was one of those neat little swivel rockers, so it was face to the window with my back to the hallway. I will add I was surprised to see my husband up before me-on a non -workday, especially with the idea all I was doing was breast-feeding and coming back to bed.

Here I am, sitting alone in a rocking chair thinking how I'm going to make the most of today as I'm not one for sulking too long. Then I hear whispers in the hallway. A familiar voice, "Happy Birthday to you." The way my mom sings those 4 words can warm your soul. I swung around in my chair to see not one, not two, but three familiar faces. My mom, Ashleigh, and Aleisha. Their faces lit up loudly, whispering surprise. All I can muster were tears. Their singing was replaced with happy tears, and we sat there, soaking up the moment. How? How did you make this happen? Ashleigh says, "We chose to show up" My sister had gotten the idea they would jump in the car and hand-deliver the birthday cake this year, and so that's what they did.

To defy reality and create magic for the ones you love. This is what purposeful living looks like. My mom said she realized time was going to pass one way or another. It would pass if she were driving or sleeping. The only thing that would change is the ending. I would be so blessed if this were just a one-time thing. This extraordinary moment was ordinary to me. It was the way of life for us. This is characteristic of our family. We get better with time. We are makers of time. We have Brave Heart for those we love. That day we made a deal to do everything in our power to be with each other on the 30th.

Circumstances change life changes. Sometimes you can't do what you want to. You can't physically show up. This is where you need Grace. Grace, for the moments you wish were possible; but you just can't make happen.

It's also a moment worth noting, just because you don't succeed at the whole thing doesn't mean you can't strive to succeed at most things. Being free to emotionally show up should never be under valued- it's what gets us through the times when we can't physically be there. I love my sisters, and I would be remiss if I didn't break my heart we couldn't follow through with this commitment. I missed Ashleigh's 30th and don't even remember the circumstances, only it was not possible to be there. We did get to be with Aleisha on hers, and it was a fun moment looking back at our 30th's knowing we chose to live and embrace life. Be a maker of time by making time for others—even just a moment to send an encouraging note.

Live on purpose.

* * *

Here are my 5 minutes to win it in your day:

Activity leads to productivity. The problem is I don't happen to be of the active type. I own a shirt that says 'indoorsy.' So, what to do? When you are actively pursuing change in your life- all signs point to start small, be consistent. My first one minute is dedicated to physical activity.

1. 1-minute plank- If you are new to planks, try 30 seconds followed by 30 seconds of stretching. I love planks because; They are highly effective at engaging the whole body. Quick and the physical act mirrors strengthening our emotional core.
2. 1 minute of mindfulness. I choose one-minute prayers, moments to focus intention on what I am creating. You choose your mindfulness.
3. 1 minute to text as many people as you can to tell them how grateful you are for them. This shifts the focus from you, making time for others.
4. 1 minute of eye contact with yourself. I know we struggle to accept being seen by others. To fully step into being seen, you must learn how to see yourself. Spend the minute looking in the mirror, acknowledging all you are doing right. Embrace being your own best friend in this one minute.
5. In my search to find moments of connection and my deep connection with gathering around the table with my family at the end of the day, making space to see each other. On days we couldn't do to schedules, I noticed I felt as though I had failed. In exploring this, I understood what I really wanted was the moment of connection. How do we create meaningful connections in one minute? EYE contact. I took one minute and divided it into sections of time for each family member. In our family, everyone gets fifteen seconds. Try this. There is no way you can hide the day when you look someone in the eyes. This builds trust. It releases oxytocin, and it stimulates the joy center in the brain. This is fifteen seconds of gathering around the table.

You can do this 5 minute to win it several times throughout the day or just once. The point is making time for change means you need a plan, and you have to do it on purpose. I hope this helps. Use the rest of this page to journal some thoughts so far, or perhaps some additional 1 minute activities you'd like to add.

Reflection space:

Twenty-Five

Fingerprints

The undeniable thing about life is...It's messy.

*S*he fiercely scrubbed it, methodically round and round, moving side to side up and down. It's the motherhood version of wax on wax off. The feeling of uselessness waves over her as she opens and closes the glass storm door inviting the sun to highlight any hint of evidence 3 adventurous boys were being contained behind it. Alas, there it was, one more smudge. With a quick swipe, she steps back, breathing in the refreshing orange and rosemary scent of the freshly polished glass door. She takes a minute because she knows it won't last. By the time she's done the back door, alas, there are new fingerprints on the front door.

This was my cycle. The day I decided I loved the fingerprints on my doors was freeing. My love of these fingerprints is exceeded only by the pure rush of giddiness reflecting on a beautifully polished glass door, dishwasher, mirror... basically anything clean.

The day I decided to love them was the day I realized their value. I was sitting there at the kitchen table when I looked out at the back door seeing all the prints. They were so thick they blurred the view. Some were long and smeared as if someone had been in a hurry. Others were clear and precise, like someone made them on purpose. Others were swirly as if someone was creating a piece of art and got interrupted. I found myself sucked in by the stories represented on the glass door. Each one was a moment in time, a conversation, a fight, a tear, a giggle, a rush of adrenalin fueling an epic escape in a game of chase. Some were accidental, while others were most definitely on purpose.

As I was mesmerized by these little fingerprints, it came over me how important they were. Their value. Collectively they are all fingerprints; what makes them unique is the stories they tell, the impact they leave behind. We are all fingerprints in the world. We can appear messy, generic, even like we are a mistake. Like we were created by accident. We can get entrapped in the perfection of cleaning up our story to improve the view. Like my rat race of chasing fingerprints with my norwex cloth, it's exhausting. It makes you avoid the sun. In case you missed a spot. Living in hiding.

Embracing Grace changes this narrative. It strips the shame and embarrassment away, leaving you free to step into the light. To shine brightly, embracing the messy.

Empowered to make your mark and Brave enough to say it's ok if I make a mess.

In this Grit meets Grace state of being, you leave a masterpiece unique only to your fingerprint on this world.

A mark only you can make and a story only you can tell. Raising Brave Hearts in each other, says I see your fingerprints, tell me your story. You may be ready to argue with me now. To justify yours is less significant _____{INSERT your excuse}.

I hear you, so let's start small.

Shortly after my epiphany, I led a devotional at church. I asked the ladies if they thought they were valuable here in our congregation. The thing about value is everyone wants to have it, but not everyone is willing to say they have it, like admitting our value might be mistaken for arrogance. This can especially and unfortunately, be seen in faith communities. In short, a world where titles equate value and purpose- your value of service in the church in the absence of a title invites the "who are you" mentality when speaking to your own value and ability to contribute.

Spontaneously following my question of value, everyone had to use the bathroom, get more food, check an urgent text message. *Desert thirst* and *famine* set in across the room as they sipped their drinks and pondered the questions. Silence is something I'm still mastering. Still uncomfortable in my own skins speaking in front of others, I interpreted the silence for disinterest. I suspect if I asked the question.

"Name someone other than yourself who has value here."

I would not have had such a quiet response. Eventually, one speaks up, then another, and a calm affirmation comes over the room as everyone begins to agree. It's terribly hard sometimes to see our own contributions as valuable. Sometimes it's as small as showing up {although I believe showing up is one of the bravest things you can do} and as BIG as launching a new ministry.

We can quickly get sucked into comparing. This creates confusion and struggle. It's close to my heart, and if I have felt this, chances are somewhere on your journey to finding yourselves have too.

I'm a visual learner, I love to create, so I merged the two for an illustration to emphasize the impact of your mark. Before the Devo, I painted a tree trunk with long, varied branches. It stretched wide and tall. I outlined a heart on the trunk, and inside I wrote the initials of our church U.H. I invited the ladies to choose a shade of green ink to place their fingerprint on one of the branches. I had 3 shades of green, light, medium, and dark. It was fun to watch them all placing their mark. That little tree barely had a branch filled. I explained, the trunk represented God as our core. The branches were all the ministry opportunities to serve.

Your fingerprint is what makes the difference. Our challenge that year was to fill the tree. To place it where we could see it as encouragement. Even if you feel unseen, IF you show up, you made your mark. Sometimes your fingerprint is the background to someone else's, they are different and unique, and that's what makes them beautiful. I had lofty goals of this growing over time and that there would be many trees around the building full of fingerprints. Someday it might happen. I am thankful over that year, we filled at least one tree.

Every time we were together, we made our fingerprint on the tree. The tree grew and was hung in one of the classrooms as a reminder. I don't get too concerned these days with messy doors. I extend lots of grace to those who **see the mess**. I link arms with those who smile at the stories they represent. I leave them around longer than necessary sometimes just to remind myself of the fingerprints I'm leaving behind in the world. The ones you can't see, the messy ones, the inspiring ones - the accidental ones. The ones I make on purpose, so you know I was here.

Those ones on purpose; those are hard. They are the ones you might see; they are the ones that call me out. They are the passions I try to negotiate and deny. They are the ones that belong to my brave heart. 'Cause, a Brave Heart is exactly what I'll need to take action. You have yours too. The moments where you think about choosing to act and the very next question is, what if I fail.

I write to share the journey of raising my own Brave Heart so together we can raise each other up. Failure is part of the journey. Making a mess is part of the message. It's all connected, and you can't; unfortunately, have one without the other. It's a big responsibility when you start waking up in the world, when things start stirring inside you, inviting you to fulfill your purpose. Make your mark, friend. When you do, I'll be there cheering for you, even if no one notices.

Twenty-Six

Birthdays Unmet Expectations

Thanks to my mom, my birthday used to be about me. Then, I had kids and I realized a birthday symbolized much more. A great act of selflessness, dedication, and sacrifice by my mom. Thank you! I wouldn't be able to enjoy this day without you.

One year for my birthday, I had said I wanted to go to dinner with friends and family. We walked in, and in the back of the restaurant, I saw a private room with pink balloons filling the room. My heart fluttered as I looked at Josh, falling in love with him all over again. I thought this man GETS me. I didn't even have to say what I really wanted!!! I didn't have to say how much I love surprise parties and I had always dreamed of being surprised for my birthday. I tried to be nonchalant.

As we "waited to be seated," I did begin to get a bit suspicious since no one was actually <u>IN</u> the party room waiting for my arrival. I shrugged off the suspicion, and convinced myself "waiting for our seats" was obviously a decoy. Waiting and waiting. Then some familiar faces began to arrive.

Trying to act surprised, I mustered a convincing, "oh, what are you doing here?" "Surprise!" he said, with a hint of sarcasm. I could tell things weren't going exactly as he had planned. Then his parents arrive, and his mom hands him flowers, which he, in turn, hands me. Surprise again. Awe, thanks, babe, they are beautiful.

"We are ready for you," the host says. We head back toward the room. Yes, my heart is fluttering now as I think here it comes, my party is about to begin.

I think there was actually an audible sound of brakes screeching as we stopped outside the room. The host turns to the forced together seating arrangement.

"Here you go. Party of 15!"

Gutted! I was literally gutted. It would have been one thing to be seated across, but right outside the party room. A sheet of glass between my real party and my dream party.

It's ok. You can laugh. I did- 5 years later. It was quite a moment. A moment I certainly didn't expect but also did. I don't remember the details of the next few moments; however, I am certain those moments weren't me, thanking my husband for inviting all our friends together for a sweet memorable evening. I'm thankful I possessed some sort of decorum not to throw a fit or pout about it, although the moment definitely felt heavy. I DO remember looking at that room and playing out the fantasy life I wished for. Imagining it was me, it was my party room. I compared my reality to another version, an unexpressed, high stakes, vulnerable version of my life I wanted but never shared. The worst part is I wanted to hold him accountable for not making it happen.

BLAME- it's a joy stealer. It takes you out of the present and thrusts you into a million versions of what could have happened, and forces you to pick someone to sacrifice as tribute to your unmet expectations.

That moment was a shaping moment. One of the many moments that lead to realizing unmet expectations will happen whether you declare your expectations or don't. At least if you say them out loud, they have the chance of coming to fruition. In the same way, I remember looking in the mirror that day and realizing once again my face didn't match my feelings; I barely recognize that version of myself, but I will never forget her. That version of me was the beginning of learning to ask.

Embracing the fear of being known and inviting people in. Dreaming again and creating a life I wish existed. That particular day revealed to me, I didn't feel known.

Friends, You can't actually LIVE your life in a corner of your mind playing out scenarios. Before a risk, we weigh the reward. Sometimes we are aware, sometimes it's automatic, maybe even routine. If it is a familiar risk, we keep taking it without always being mindful of the choice.

In some cases, the ability to {choose} fades, the lines blur, and we forget we are active participants. This is most common in relationships, behavior becomes predictable, and we assume our roles. For better or worse, we take comfort in phrases like "You can't teach an old dog new tricks," as acceptable wisdom for settling into our lives. We say it's idealistic to have our spouse meet our requests. We say our kids are "Just kids," we lower our standards for meaningful friendship and avoid challenging norms.

I don't believe we do this on purpose, and I suppose that's the point. We aren't embracing purpose-driven lives. I am not referring to an epiphany you had in the dark of night which revealed a master plan for you. I'm speaking of living a deliberate life. A present, on purpose life; crafting each relationship. So why don't we? **FEAR**

The fear -if you SHARE, they won't CARE.

In sharing this story with people throughout the years, I often get this question and statement.

- "But what if they just don't do it?"
- "If you have to tell them, it doesn't mean the same."

If you're thinking this too, I am hugging you right now. I'm also challenging you to change your thinking. I'm inviting you to shift your thinking to embrace the fear of vulnerability and be brave enough to share your hopes and dreams with at least one person. If they make it happen because you ASKED, I suggest it IS loving, and IT ABSOLUTELY means something. In many ways, it almost means more. It says you saw me when I was vulnerable, you listened to my dreams, you protected my heart, and when the timing was right. You lifted me up.

Before you object, I need to say, it's not the only kind of love. It's ONE kind of love! It's a fulfilling kind of love that comes from a place of being complete. It's a kind you can only offer when you are willing to risk it all. It's challenging. It takes vulnerability, and it demands trust. It changes you.

Brave Hearts are willing to risk being seen. They trust their people and love deeply.

* * *

Our dryer was out for the fourth time that summer. I convinced myself I was getting in touch with my inner pioneer woman. However, I was growing weary of spending every day hanging laundry on the line. Juggling, feeding my kids, and checking the weather. I'm taking this opportunity to acknowledge what life was like before dryers. WOW, did those Momma's crush it. Salute!

Anyway, It was my birthday, and our sweet supper club was hosting me for dinner. Are you ready to go? Josh asked… Yup, as soon as this last load washes, I want to use Alison's dryer. We have those friends that let you bring your laundry over, all kinds of laundry, and they don't judge. It's a sweet and cherished friendship. We pull in, and I recognize other friends parked in the driveway. I wave and say, "Oh, wow!" I didn't know she invited them to supper club. It's not uncommon for us to invite extra friends over, and I love this about our crew. The kids bail out of the car, and I begin to get the laundry out of the trunk.

Josh swiftly places his hand on mine, not tonight. Just leave it. Let's go in first, and then I'll come out later. I'd like to say I said, "Thank you, dear,"…but instead, I let a few stories drift into my head. I made it about him thinking it was inappropriate to carry in our laundry in front of other people. I protested. *"It's just (naming friends), and I don't want sour clothes."* He insisted, *"I said, Leave it."*

My face turned a bit sour. Rolling my eyes, I muttered something like... *"I hate that you care what people think."*

I'm greeted by our friend, "Are you ok?" my expressions are noticeable.

"NOPE!" ('cause remember I am radically, totally truth-telling now). He steps aside, extending his arm as though he's clearing the way for me and my attitude. I walk in, and I AM SPEECHLESS.

There. They. Are. All of our friends. Balloons, pineapples, details everywhere...

Then she says, "we channeled our inner you. I hope you like it." LIKE IT? I love it. This amazing tribe of Brave Hearts came together to throw me the surprise party of my dreams. My first words were to my husband as I pivoted around. He was grinning a mix between Gotcha, and you should have trusted me. I poured out I'm sorry's, and we laughed. When you screw up, you can spend the night defending yourself and picking it apart, or you can say "oops" and transition into the best moments. The moments after you right a wrong. The forgiveness. *"Thank you for forgiving me."* I mouth.

We had such a great night with amazing food and hospitality. I felt so honored, and it was a moment to embrace. Living on purpose takes time. It was nearly a decade later I was living out my dream surprise party. It wasn't so much getting what I wanted. It was about the journey to developing relationships with people who care deeply about living your best life moments. They are champions for raising brave hearts, and the best part is...It's just who they are. Not in the accident kind of way, in the ON PURPOSE kind of way. They plug in and engage. They risk being seen, and they love without judging. They are my people, my family.

The world will try to pull you apart from EVERYONE you love, always be fighting to get back to each other. The journey back to each other, the choice you make to live on purpose, is what makes up your life together.

Circumstances change, life changes. Sometimes you can't do what you want to. This is where you need grace. It's not a reason to hide.

You must set the intention for who you will be WHEN life gets crazy, not if. You must stand in the great expectations you have for life and keep sharing. Keep telling the truth. Keep asking for what you want. I know it's scary. It was for me too. I felt silly and selfish. The world is not served by you playing small. Learning to share the desires of your heart leads to being fully known and strong, honest relationships. KEEP SHARING.

Reflection space:

Twenty-Seven

Real Ingredients

B rave Heart has to have real ingredients ALL the time. It cannot survive in any other conditions besides authentic living. THAT's hard, which is why you are brave. I am a bit of a one-hit-wonder in the kitchen. I rarely use recipes, and the book I do get recipes from is tattered and falling apart. IT IS SACRED. If any goodwill soul ever sneaks it off to mend it as a surprise, they may also meet their demise. Hands off for real. I digress. I think people who know me best would say,

"She views recipes as more of a guide. The rest is all heart."

I've lost count of the times I have been asked for the recipe, and I have to admit there isn't really a recipe AND if I try to recreate it, it will likely be different. Side note it is also fun to know each dish is unique. This process is also a source of conflict in my little, big heart. I never want to make someone feel less than. Sometimes one of the downsides to sharing your talents is others think, man, I could never... I know this to be true because I was that way once upon a time. I saw people doing things I didn't think I could do. I compared my style to theirs and thought I was lacking.

When I shifted to being inspired and empowered by the talent around me, encouraging others, it became easier to share my own talents. Prior to learning this, I would either never hand out the recipe OR meticulously try to recreate it prior to giving it to them.

I'm sure your thinking - WHY DON'T YOU JUST USE THE RECIPE. Save myself the headache, right? I wish I could. It's just not my style. Sorry, not sorry. I can't think of a recipe I have used exactly as it is written except for my mother's pavlova, which was given to her by a dear friend. She was taught how to make it because it is a show-up kind of dessert. There are a few desserts I know how to make because I was shown how not because of a recipe. They are relationship desserts, the kind you have to show up for.

WOW, are they worth it? Yes, they take time, but they take time because they are worth it. I love baking and cooking. It's like a slow dance between creating a meal and being inspired by new flavors. I feel like food should come together in one amazing bite, not leave you chasing a flavor. It's one of my therapies for sure, and don't get me started on frosting cookies. THAT is something I hold near and dear. I bake my own batch just to ensure I have plenty. Kids get theirs. I get mine.

Before you think Martha Stewart is my mother, let me say I am for sure not opposed to a semi-homemade meal or pizza Friday. I just have high value for quality ingredients and don't mind the extra time to make it extra special. Pies will always be better with homemade crust and fresh whip cream, rolls will be better with butter over margarine, and real mash potatoes are still a must. My hubby nicknamed me the food snob because of my elevated preferences. I am utterly peeved when I request butter at a restaurant and get margarine. Or ask if it's real whip cream and its cool whip. I feel cheated like I thought I was getting something real and got a fake substitute instead.

My love of REAL things is confined to food. I am hungry for authentic people. Trust and vulnerability are a lost art these days. In our Insta-world, our culture is scrambling for the next filter to enhance beauty and lessen the imperfections. I'm not saying I don't love a fun filter. I just don't want to hide behind it. Pretending to be something you are not robs you of meaningful connection. Using real ingredients to grow your Brave Heart is as meaningful as a good cup of tea and a slice of pavlova. It's the foundation of the relationship you nurture. A Brave Heart is a heart that shows up. It's a heart that says; yeah, I'm a little messy, and I don't have all the things figured out yet, but I am here. Let's build a real relationship, with real ingredients, based on mutual trust. If you are struggling to recall a relationship like this, start with yourself. Start being your own BFF. Be honest. Start feeding your heart REAL truths. When you start being honest with yourself, it's easier, to be honest with others.

Finally, we love to host parties and share unique foods with friends. It's a love language of sorts. It's not about showing off. It's how I say you're worth my time, and I love you. Thank you to all my friends who come by for a chat and good food. Thank you for letting me cook for you, and thank you for being made of real ingredients.

Twenty-Eight

Let's go to Paris

~❦~

W hat happens when you spend so much time creating a life, molding it, making choices, spending money? When your *plans* don't turn out like you planned them. What then? Do you get to change your mind? Do you *get* to start over?

When I was a little girl, my parents went on a trip to Paris. I imagined how exotic it must have been, and I longed for a trip of my own. When they returned, my mother was sporting a new perfume, and after MANY conversations about how I would like to go there, she said, "when you're 16, we will go." She might as well have said next week. I latched on to that promise. As the years went by, her perfume served as a gentle reminder, Paris was drawing near.

Here's the thing about *Promises;* Sometimes, as life goes on, the circumstance under which you gave the promised change. What then? What's the difference between a dream and a promise? Do you give yourself- and others permission to reimagine?

When my mother made this promise, she didn't foresee the move from Scotland to the United States. In Scotland, we could have taken the Euro Rail for a short trip under the sea. The move to the States, while exciting and new; Also left me feeling *less than* hopeful as my 16th birthday approached.

Years of anticipation had led to this birthday, and yet Paris looked as though it would have to wait.

THEN a Miracle! A Last-minute value deal, a likely never before or since kind of deal. Viola- 2 tickets to Paris coming right up.

Friday; No Paris...Monday, Au Revoir. Really! It was just THAT fast. Mom and I were finally going to Paris. It was simply glorious, glamorous, and everything a 15-almost 16-year-old could possibly wish for. I gushed to my friends. I couldn't for the life of me understand why they weren't happy for me {insert eye roll} ... My boyfriend was less than excited too. Turns out when my mom pleaded with me to take pictures WITHOUT his letter jacket on, "you know, just in case you don't stay together forever." she was right.

My years of dreaming about the perfume scented golden streets of Paris were finally about to come true. I was sure the music there just hung in the air effortlessly as if it belonged there. The food...The Romance. Remember, I'm 16 with a boyfriend and had seen PLENTY of gushy romance movies. Everything magical always seemed to happen in Paris. My mother is a romantic at heart, filled with nothing but the best of intentions. Creating memories is one of the things she does well. Our adventure was waiting...

* * *

As we got off the train, smells fill my senses. A mixture of fresh bread and wine. I found myself thinking, 'Where is the limo, where in the world is our hotel, and for heaven's sake, where is the Eiffel Tower.' {it's ok you can laugh; my inner monolog is quite dramatic}.

I just knew the hotel we were staying in would have the most excellent view of the Eiffel Tower, the arch de triumph, and the river. It's worth pointing out if you've ever been to Paris, you will know this is quite impossible.

As we weave through traffic on foot, jerking our suitcases filled with *shoes* and *hope*, we pass by a quaint corner market and bakery. I think at least we will have something to eat. Another thing begins to annoy me. Turns out my "fluent" French I learned to speak in primary school and tea parties wasn't quite so "*fluent* "- it was basically useless. What language *is* this? Everywhere

I looked, they spoke way too fast. No one asked me my name, what time it was, my favorite color, or where I lived. Useless, I tell you- it was all useless.

We finally made it to our Hotel. This hotel was motel 8 level. Pictures did not do it justice and not in a good way. It *was* clean and efficient, so it met the need. Flopping on the bed, I let out a sigh. The reality of the day was heavy. Jet lag wrapped in unmet expectations make for an interesting combo. I rolled over and made my way to the window. Sliding the curtain to one side, I look at the streets below. People bustling in their ordinary lives, which to me seemed extraordinary.

How privileged they were to live ordinarily in such a magical place. It was a strange moment for me as I realized to them...this was just another day, for me; today was a privilege. As I stared at the streets below, I wrestled with the guilt of knowing I should be thankful and feeling very disappointed. Have you ever had a moment like that?

"Mom?" I finally muster, without breaking my stare. "I don't want to sound ungrateful, but this is not the Paris I was looking for or imagined." As a mother myself now, I am certain The Holy Spirit grabbed her tongue and silenced her!

"Mom?" I turned to see if she was still in the room. She came closer to the window and reached out to hold me, a patient look sweeping over her face.

"Let's take a rest. Then after, let's go find the Paris you're looking for."

This moment was my normal. It was what I would have expected her to say. She is a dreamer and listener, and creator of dreams. Only as I grew from a young girl into a woman did I realize how extraordinary this moment truly was. How shaping of my life it was. How it taught me to pursue your heart's desire. I learned you can decide at any moment you don't like where you are, and then you can go find what you do want. You can create what you wish existed. Here's the rest of the story- It's better if you do it together.

After our rest, we dressed for dinner and went bravely into the city to seek moments matching our dreams. I want you to hear in your hearts...WE WENT OUT. We took action. We did not sit in our hotel room, ruminating on all the disappointment. We didn't quit.

Most people you'll meet will say Paris is dirty. Yes, it is true, but I didn't see any of it. I was too busy looking for all the moments of sparkling joy. When we made it to the Eiffel Tower, it was as if all the magic of the movies was there waiting for us. Street performer and music hung in the air. Smells of fresh fruit and crepes. I can't tell you how many steps are to the top of the Eiffel Tower or Notre Dame, but I can tell you the view is worth it. The view is what I remember. WE found a rooftop garden to stroll through, took a nap in the park with the most perfect weather you could imagine. We ate Pear Sorbet in a 3 story Hagen Daz parlor. Sacre'- Coeur Cathedral is worth the climb, standing tall at the city's highest point. Its' breathtaking beauty processed a stillness, living up to its' name Sacre'- Coeur Basilica- The Sacred Heart of Paris.

It was the trip of a lifetime. It also had the potential to be a disappointment of a lifetime. There were so many opportunities for things to go differently. It took both of us showing up and willing to share our dreams; To go together. While I can't gift you a trip to Paris, I can gift you this moment to remember. Right now. You can use my story. You can decide to go find the version of your life you're dreaming about. You can go find your Paris. You will need to be brave, you will need each other, and you can't give up until you find it. I'll be here cheering you on. I believe in you.

Someone's ordinary is someone else's extraordinary! Remember this when you're tempted to complain about your ordinary life. Together we can raise up a community of Brave Hearts who don't quit. They change what they see. They dare to expand their vision for life and then pursue it with passion. They fight for each other's dreams and lift each other up so they can see better.

They embrace someone's ordinary is someone else's extraordinary.

Twenty-Nine

Time to Say Goodbye

⟡

Brave Heart knows when to let go and say goodbye. I took 6 months off writing this book because of what someone said to me. I know, I know. I've spent all this time encouraging you not to stop being you because of others' opinions.

I was getting to the point where I was speaking my intentions out loud. I was comfortable with saying I'm writing a book on Raising Brave Hearts. At a workshop, I attended we had been doing some work on releasing things which hold you back. I was raw and vulnerable.

"I'm writing a book about being brave and my journey. I want to encourage others with my story."

"Be careful," he said.

"BE careful you don't invite another generation of struggle. Be careful you don't teach your kids a life of conquering struggles."

I felt so misunderstood in the moment. Why would I do that? That would be horrible. I want more for my kids. I want more for you.

It consumed me for days. I ruminate over it. Wrestled with it. Was he right? I went back to my journals and poured over them for evidence he was wrong. It was a tough few months. I was blinded by his words, stumbling around in the darkness in search of an answer.

During those months, I wrote every reflection I had on this concept of inviting struggle, I had couch talks with friends. I prayed. It was frustrating. If it were a snake, it would have bitten me. Right there, hiding in plain sight. I'm so comforted to affirm I didn't need to learn anything *NEW*; just apply some awareness and distinction. I hushed the noise around the message.

So here it is.

1. YOU can do hard things. You do not need to make things hard to earn the right to move on. Sounds totally easy and a no-brainer, right? Um, no. Look around. It is possible to be brave and not have brave to be your identity. We live in a world where we draw strength from the title overcomers, built to survive. Sometimes it can be easy to identify being as brave as the same thing and think we are nothing without it. Don't create a life which invites struggle but know you can move through it when presented with it. Brave Hearts are not jumping around, inviting ourselves into problem-solving. Rather when a problem presents, we are willing to look for solutions.

2. There will always be distractions. I finished writing this in one of the busiest seasons of my life. In a pandemic where most of the world was wishing the year away, I wanted something good. You'll know you're in distraction mode when it looks like you're doing it, but what you're doing doesn't produce results. Organizing my pages looks like working on my book. Thinking about ideas looks like work. Living in the opinion of others about the topic I choose to write looks like work.

3. Deciding it's getting published by X date- getting up at 4 am to write this, finding the 'AND' moments. I can both promote a product launch *and* a book *and* a workshop at the same time *and* fulfill my other responsibilities. This is deciding it will be done, all of it.

4. How did I do all of it? I'm not going to tell you to give up TV, mostly because every time I read "successful people do watch TV" in a self-help book, I immediately feel like a failure. I'm just asking you consider growing your vision of what you want to be so big there is no room for

any other distractions. You will not want to watch tv when you know it's time away for fulfilling your dreams.

5. In the same way if it were your last day on earth, you wouldn't spend it making excuses. You wouldn't spend it worrying about money. If you wouldn't spend your day worrying, delaying, avoiding...why spend today there. Grow your vision for what is possible.

✳ ✳ ✳

Quick exercise.

Get a piece of paper now or you can use the reflection space below. (don't wait until you're at the store to get that cute notebook you are now inspired to get to write all your dreams in-. I did this once, so I know you).

Grab the first writing tool you can find.

Write what I wish existed in the middle of the page. The only rule is you ask yourself this one question before writing anything else. IF time and resources were unlimited, what would life look like?

Draw a line and then write one thing you wish existed in your life now.

If this is your first time doing something like this, it will feel weird. This exercise will likely feel Embarrassing, and you'll want to grab a heart-shaped padlock for a box and lock it away. DON'T - remember we now care what others think, but we don't let their opinions choose for us.

Do not negotiate with yourself. This vision needs to invite you to laugh when you look at it. To scare you a little and to humble you. We don't get anywhere in life without a team. Without others. I will speak to our journey together forever. I believe this to my core.

Steps to putting it all together:

1. Get organized. Not your laundry, your dreams. Once you've dared to dream, you've got to write it down. Organization is just the steps to making the dream a reality. Once you've got your steps, you've got your path. What's it going to take to get you from "Meh" to "Yeah" about your life. Don't get overwhelmed. It's just a checklist.
2. Ask for help! Share your dreams and invite others to help you. Together is better, and you'd be surprised who is just waiting to cheer you on.

You must embrace saying goodbye to the need to defend what you want for your life to others'. You might have to defend it to yourself, even rest to reflect and get clarity. When you *really* decide to move forward; You are the only one you need permission from. Say goodbye to the excuses and elevate *why* you want change.

Reflection space:

Thirty

What Next

꧁꧂

We've been on quite a journey so far. I hope that by now, you have a sense of what a brave heart looks like, and you've begun to recognize yours. The "Raising" part always gets everyone. Why Raising Brave Hearts? Are you writing a book about raising your kids? No, that's the next one. This is why I chose Raising Brave Hearts.

> **"Be B R A V E enough to**
> **create the life you wish existed."**

Raising brave hearts in our families and communities is dear to me. We all know the feeling you get when life hands you *less* than inspiring circumstances. If we are ever to rise above our less than moments, we've got to dare to dream. Be brave enough to create what we wish existed, then invite others to join us. This is one of the mindsets I want to foster in my children.

Landon came home from school one day. He was conflicted about how to solve a problem. At first, he decided to *just do* nothing. After a moment of rest, I asked

"what would be your very best, yes. If you could have the best of both, how would you go about getting it?"

"Well, that's impossible. There is no way you can do that, MOM!" -It's tough feeling stuck.

"Son, the question wasn't, is it possible? The question was, what **if** it were possible? Dream a little, give a voice to what you would change, what you want to be different."

See, he was experiencing a loss even when he didn't know a loss had occurred. The disappointment can be cumulative over time if we don't have the tools to notice it. He began to be silly and sarcastic with his answers as only a sixth-grader can.

"Fine, I wish the whole world would give me what I want!"

"What if you can't have everything you want? Who will you be? What will you create as your solution?"

> *I want them always to know YOU can create what you wish existed, even if what you are creating is a new way of responding to disappointment.*

"What's your **and** moment?" I nudged.

"I want to be able to do both," he replied.

I want them to learn you don't have to settle for wishing you felt different about something or had different circumstances. There is always something to create, again even if the *something* is not a change in circumstances but a change in how you feel. Most of the time, it's not the event we desperately want to change. It's how we *feel* about what happened we want relief from.

"Great, now let's look at what it would take to have both and see who we can invite to help us create the solution."

I want them to learn how to advocate for themselves by sharing their goals and asking for help.

That situation, created an '**and**' moment for him. He enlisted the people around him to help him accomplish what he had been hoping for. I was so proud of him for getting unstuck.

They say it takes a village to raise a family. I say it takes a *family* to raise a community. A family who will raise each other's Brave Hearts and chooses the 'And' moments so they can create what they wish existed. Many people doing a little bit, together making an impact for good.

Brave is the spirit you nurture inside you. It's the heart of a dreamer that has been disappointed but doesn't stop dreaming. It's seeing the whole of someone, not their brokenness. It's crazy like a child who says, "I'm gonna be a YouTuber with a million followers," because no one said he couldn't. It's doing it without all the answers. It's hope, faith, and belief. Taking responsibility for the change you want to see. Taking action is the "raising." The change in you creates an impact with massive ripples.

So Be brave enough to create the life you wish existed.

Imagine a world where your word was your bond. People meant what they said and said what they meant. Where people said, " I trust you," not "prove yourself."

Now imagine we lived in a world where we were free to be with the people who matter when it matters; because we live in a world where PEOPLE matter. We did more for each other, not less. We gave **not** on merit, but with blind abundance; because who we **choose** to be matters ALL the time, not just when people are looking or when they deserve our kindness. Imagine you created life by design, not default. And in **that** life, you could, in fact, make a difference. YOU could make the world a better place.

I live in a world where I believe it's possible. I believe *you* can too. I know it will not happen overnight, but it will happen.

How do I know? Because I know how much it means to me my children have a future like this and because I want it for you too. I know how much it meant reclaiming my own heart and raising Brave Hearts in my home. I know how much I want you to embrace yours. When we are motivated by WHY's which change and inspire us; we know FEAR of loss is not part of the journey.

My friend Susan gifted me this poem when I shared the vision for Raising Brave Hearts. Thank you Susan.

I hold space for those who believe
What they dream of they'll receive

I help process Forward teaching,
Raising Brave Hearts for a new reaching.

Finding gaps and filling in,
Serving up YOUR greatest win.

Susan Kay Dahl

Epilogue

"Please don't go Momma" Those are words you NEVER want to hear your child say. Especially when the next words you have to say are; "Son, I can't promise you I'll be able to stay. All I can give you is a moment to talk about what comes next. What happens if I die." I have only shared this story with a few, there were no Facebook posts. In fact, the only post was of success. Pictures of my boys and their dad at the peak of the climb to the top. The only missing was me. I had insisted the other boys and Josh go-ahead. I planned to walk with our youngest and my sister. The play by play is LONG, there were many moments to ask ourselves, "Why are we doing this." Moments to feel shame about the mistakes we made that day in the canyon. It quickly became clear, this was not going to be the day we expected.

That summer there was a heat surge in the canyon we were hiking. The temperature soared to over 115 degrees. We thought we were prepared, we had a plan. Then the plan went terribly wrong. We lost contact with the rest of our group and I found myself experiencing a heat stroke. As I lay there on the ground ants crawling all over my skin, all I could feel was this longing for just one more minute. My oldest son and my sister sat with me praying for help to arrive in time. Here's the thing about being faced with the possibility you're about to have no more minutes on your timer. A flood of what-ifs consumes you. All the things you thought you'd have more time for. I asked Landon to go check if he could see help coming, as we had sent for help over an hour ago.

"Get him what he needs. Don't let my kids wonder what I was like, promise

148

me you won't stop telling them stories about me." I pleaded with my sister to promise me.

"I promise," she said. God knew who I needed by my side in that moment. I don't know how she stayed so calm, so consistent. She was amazing.

Landon made it back with the news he couldn't see any signs of help. As my heart rate continued to soar and I began struggling to stay conscious, I wanted to hide from the pain I was feeling. The fear of the moment. I wanted to promise him I wasn't going to die every time he said, "Momma! keep your eyes open, talk to me." Talk to him? What do you say in a moment like this? All I could think about was what if I don't make it. What do I want him to know. I decided to tell him about what comes next.

"Landon, I have to share something with you, no Momma ever wants to say to her kids. I have to prepare you for what happens if I don't get to have anymore tomorrows with you. If I die." You can not imagine the conflict I felt in saying those words to him. The crisis of the moment. The only thing that mattered to me was him having better tools than I did. It was important to me he knew where to get answers and he knew I had prepared letters for them. "You know how I've been writing a lot? Well, I have letters and journals full of ideas about life. Stories about you and how much I love you. Things I want you to know, things you're not ready for yet, but someday will be. I need you to know how to find those."

If you're thinking I'm strange because I have goodbye letters to my kids, it's ok. They are completion letters. I have had many a health scare in my life, each leaving me with the feeling of borrowed time. While I don't wish ill health on anyone, I do wish the feeling of borrowed time for you. To be faced with a moment such as this creates focus and intention. It leaves you wanting to leave a legacy for those who come after so there will be no question of what you stood for. How big you loved.

We spent those moments in waiting, talking about his questions. It was beautiful in its sacred way. To have a moment like that is not one you go looking for, but embrace it when you do. He embraced it too. He was strong but vulnerable. Honest and brave. My favorite moment following all we had to say. In the quiet, I hear this most innocent voice full of courage and confidence as he sang out. "Our God is an awesome God. He reigns from heaven above with wisdom, power, and love. Our God is an awesome God."

He chose to praise and be thankful in a moment of fear and uncertainty. He embraced his Brave Heart. My son had to grow up more than he should have that summer, but as we drove out of the canyon after being rescued by the park rangers, I caught his eyes as he looked my way. He said, "It's funny how you don't really notice someone or appreciate them until you think about them not being here anymore, I love you, Mom."

"I love you too Landon," both of us honoring the gratitude of what we had just been through.

Coming through the experience I knew I had put it off too long waiting for the perfect moment. The "IT" being all the things. We can become so complacent with taking action. Even when we have journeyed through the heartache to the other side and embrace our healing. In the following days I had so many thoughts. I imagined how different this day would look if I wasn't here. Instead of grabbing our favorite donuts, Josh would be calling our favorite people to share the news. This urgency inside me began to swell. A gift of time. When people respond to the intensity with which I live life, as "Wow you're busy." They are right. Busy is my blessing and I'm not wasting a moment of it.

"The gifts in life are not in enjoying all the times you got it right.

The GIFT is the <u>time</u> to get it right."

Cheers to you and your Brave Heart, may you capture moments of intention like fireflies on a summer night. See them for the wonder they are and with them create a life you love with the people you love.

Afterword

They say you are a reflection of your experiences...

Yikes! If this is true, I reject the notion. Life has afforded me many experiences, some less than and some more than expected. Some of the *less than* experiences I have been through; the choices I have made...I wouldn't want to be seen.

In taking responsibility for the reflection, I learned *I decide* what I see when I look in the mirror. Will I see pain and incomplete loss? Or will it be a reflection of gratitude having completed the pain, gleaning from each moment an opportunity to choose what comes next?

I choose the gratitude, forgiveness and living complete. I believe that the best quality of life can be lived when you are living forward. Life is a gift, I don't intend on wasting it.

Blessings to you and those you call yours.

Until next time, from one Brave Heart to another,

Cheers!

Jessica

About the Author

Jessica Broadway currently lives in Nixa, Missouri, with her husband and three boys. A champion for the people, she is an enthusiast for life and loves to see others rise. Jessica finds joy in telling stories about what she notices in the world. Making hard things user-friendly, she draws on her experiences growing up in Scotland, UK. Her time spent abroad inspired her to help connect people through adversity and difference.

Her strong faith in Christ Jesus guides her as she shares stories about noticing how He shows up in her life and her journey in ministry.

Jessica is a consultant specializing in guiding individuals through areas of their life they desire a transformation.

From parenting and relationships to entrepreneurship and team building. Her experience as a Grief Recovery Specialist, wife, mother, entrepreneur, PTA leader, program developer, and public speaker allows her to coach from a place of authenticity and application. She has the privilege of standing in the gap for others to believe that they can create the life they wish existed.

Our Next Steps:

Thank you for reading Raising Brave Hearts. Did you enjoy it? I'd love you to write a review and consider sharing this book with someone you know who needs encouragement to raise their Brave Heart.

Now that you've heard my story, I'd love to hear yours. How do you use your Brave Heart?Connect with me on social media or send me a message on my blog. Not ready to share yet? Need a little coaching and encouragement? Join our Raising Brave Hearts club to continue the journey.

I promise to keep cheering for you and bringing you the best tools for the journey.

Find me on social media by searching: Jessica Broadway or @themommy-bossx3

For a complete list of workshops available, check out Jessicabroadway.com

You can connect with me on:
- https://jessicabroadway.com
- https://www.facebook.com/themommybossx3
- https://www.facebook.com/livingforwardtoday
- https://www.instagram.com/themommybossx3